To the kids
of Livingston
central!

Rudy

AIMING HIGH

AIMING **HIGH**

HOW A PROMINENT SPORTS AND CELEBRITY AGENT HIT BOTTOM AT THE TOP

by **DARREN PRINCE**
with **KRISTEN MCGUINESS**

Foreword by Earvin "Magic" Johnson

LIGHT HUSTLER

Light Hustler
1601 Vine St.
Los Angeles, CA 90038
www.lighthustler.com/publishing

Printed in the United States of America.

ISBN-13: 978-1-73250-080-8

Further Praise for Darren Prince and *Aiming High*

"You will find Darren to be a force to reckon with. In spite of his prowess, a more powerful process nearly claimed him as it has so many. Now that same spirit, fully engaged in a program of recovery, is thriving and inspiring others to join in something greater. *Aiming High* shows how he got there."

Dr. Drew Pinsky, Addiction Specialist
and creator of *Celebrity Rehab*

"It's been a pleasure getting to work with and know Darren the past 15 years. *Aiming High* is very inspiring and shows us all it's never too late to make changes in ourselves."

Roy Jones Jr., Pound for Pound Boxing King
and Nine-time World Champion

"To go from being such a prominent figure in the nightlife scene to such an outspoken advocate in recovery is no easy transition, but Darren Prince has done it. *Aiming High* is a testament to a man whose journey defies logic."

Noah Tepperberg, co-owner, Tao Group

"Darren Prince does everything with passion—whether it's nurturing his relationships, blowing up his business, or committing himself to his recovery. *Aiming High* shows that you can always change everything."

Jason Strauss, co-owner, Tao Group

"Darren and I accomplished history together when our friends and clients, Muhammad Ali and Joe Frazier, reunited in 2002 after eight years of us working together behind the scenes to make it happen. This was one of the most significant accomplishments for us both. Together, we did many great things personally and professionally. It saddened me to learn of the years of suffering Darren endured with his addictions and not being able to open up to me about them. However, it's amazing for me to reflect back now on what he accomplished, and I'm very proud of him and this incredible story."

Harlan Werner, Sports Placement Services

"I've known Darren for many, many years, and he's one of the best people I've met in the business. Yes, Darren has been successful representing athletes and celebrities for close to 25 years, but to me it's his journey through spiritual sobriety and helping others that's his biggest accomplishment."

Larry Rudolph, Music Manager
and Entertainment Entrepreneur

"Throughout Darren's spectacular career, I have been with him for his highs and his lows. The one thing, however, that has remained constant is his loyalty, dedication, and love for his family, friends, and superstar clients. I am confident that his journey will continue to be just as fruitful, sharing his message of hope and recovery with those in need. *Aiming High* is that message."

Ryan Schinman, Entertainment Marketing Guru

"Darren Prince is a recovery rock star. His story pushes the limits on what's possible on the other side of addiction. Inspiring, witty, and brutally honest...*Aiming High* is a must read."

Ryan Hampton, Recovery Advocate and Author of *American Fix: Inside the Opioid Addiction Crisis—and How to End It*

"*Aiming High* is a wild ride. Darren Prince is the quintessential story of redemption and success. I'm proud to call him a friend."

Garrett Hade, Recovery Advocate

"Darren is a person who followed his dreams and built not only a top notch marketing business but a high end drug addiction. His life's success was almost taken all away, but the gift of recovery came in. Today, Darren is what long term recovery is all about. The success within leads to the outward success. I am blessed to have him in my circle of life."

Tim Ryan, Author, star of A&E's *Dope Man*, Speaker

"Darren Prince courageously speaks his powerful truth of redemption from the leading cause of death in America for those under fifty. Resulting from the shame associated with addiction, most of those affected stay quiet, hidden, and marginalized. In *Aiming High*, Darren does what he always has done, he breaks the mold."

Greg Williams, Filmmaker of *The Anonymous People* & EVP of Facing Addiction with NCADD

"I first met Darren in February of 1992. He was sitting in front of me during the Super Bowl game in Minneapolis. He was with some friends that I knew, and immediately I felt that bond of friendship that has lasted for more than 25 years and that will last a lifetime. I was fortunate to be there on the sideline of the creation of his amazing ride by introducing him to a couple of celebrity relationships of mine, and with attention, caring respect, nurturing, and commitment, he made a spectacular career out of it, creating a unique model of representation by being a friend and agent to the iconic figures of our time. I am humbled to think that I might have had a remote part of his success! Darren is the kind of person that never says no and is the first one to always lend a helping hand. Throughout the years, I saw him grow from a young adult to a sophisticated, business savvy, and generous human being. Even though he suffered a few bumps on the road of his journey, he stayed true to himself, and with his dedication and strong will he overcame his challenges. Nonetheless his heart has never changed, with the help and unconditional love of his amazing foundation of family and friends. Darren is a star in his own right and will always have my love and support. I am proud to have him call me his friend!"

Jeff Hamilton, celebrity designer

"I knew Darren in the late nineties. He represented some of the best athletes in the world, and to outsiders, he portrayed great success. He was a man to look up to, someone I aspired to be like. I had no idea he was struggling with the demons of addiction. Seeing him today, I have met a better Darren, a more improved, passionate, and caring man. The man I once thought I knew is completely transformed, and as they say, the "best version of himself." I am so proud of his accomplishments and his selfless actions to help others struggling with alcoholism and addiction. I truly believe the work he is doing is saving lives."

Joe Tuttle, CEO of Banyan Treatment Centers

"Darren's a testament to a 12-step program. He gives his gift away to others in need and in turn keeps his for himself. I'm happy to be his sober brother and very proud of his 10 years of sobriety."

Stephen Della Valle, Turning Point Inc., Rehab Management

"Darren is the big brother I always wanted. He has always been that man that bounces back from anything. This was just a little roadblock in life, and I'm so happy he is able to share his story with the world."

Nick Cordasco, entertainment agent

"Darren is the most non-judgmental person I know... He's a great friend and is always there when you need a lift... I admire the steps he has taken in his recovery, and I love him dearly."

Chris "Vo" Volo, Prince Marketing Group-Sports and entertainment representation

"One of the few people that I typically haven't had to worry about over the years is Darren. He exudes confidence, navigates problems with the precision of a surgeon, and there are too many examples of his business acumen and success to count. However, the one time I truly saw Darren brought to his knees in submission was during his battle with drug addiction. I believe that his recovery is his biggest success, and he now most clearly resembles again that first friend I met when I moved to New Jersey at the age of 10—one who is fiercely loyal, one who puts others first, and one who is a dreamer and an optimist. I'm fairly certain I've never seen Darren happier and in a better position to help others."

Steven Simon, Prince Marketing Group-Sports and entertainment representation

"I have had the privilege of being a business partner of Darren's since day one, some 35 years ago, but more importantly his friend. I have witnessed his rise to the top of the industry while at the same time experiencing his darkest hours. To see Darren now back at the top of his game—the most important one, the game of life—is a truetestament of his will and strength. To watch him overcome everything and give back every day is an inspiration to everyone around him and will give others strength and courage to get back their lives. And that is the greatest gift of all."

Frank Basile, Business Associate

FOREWORD BY
EARVIN "MAGIC" JOHNSON

Darren and I have worked together for 23 years. During that time, he has worked 24/7, negotiating memorabilia signings, speaking engagements, appearances, and other services. It's an honor to write the foreword for his book.

Transitioning from being a renowned athlete to a successful businessman was not easy, and I like working with people who are trustworthy, motivated, and efficient. Darren was all of the above. After the second time working together for one of my signings, Darren told me that his parents were downstairs in the hotel lobby and asked if they could join us. Meeting Darren's parents helped me realize how important family was to him. His business wasn't about making money; it was about building relationships and growing extended family. He made me a part of his family, and he became a part of mine.

Two years later, Darren shared his dream to become an agent and start Prince Marketing Group. He was young, but he had a plan and he knew what he wanted to do in life. I wanted Darren to be more than successful, so I continued as his client. Over the next few years, I watched as he worked with some of the biggest stars in sports and entertainment, such as Smokin' Joe Frazier, Muhammad Ali, Pamela Anderson, Chevy Chase, Larry Bird, Dennis Rodman, Hulk Hogan, and many, many others.

As good friends, in 2006 Darren talked to me about very challenging times that he was undergoing, the most challenging being an opioid addict. "Earvin," he said, "I can't get out of bed in the morning or function during the day without painkillers. It's taken over my life. Talking, traveling, working out, eating; I can't do anything without the pills. I can't stop."

Nothing was bigger than the painkillers that he was addicted to, which were slowly taking his life. I had seen too many lives destroyed from addiction and knew he needed to get his life in order. It took some time for Darren to reach complete sobriety. After almost nearly losing his life to opioids, Darren overcame the addiction and built a greater life through his recovery. Through sobriety, he has continued to expand his business, and he is using his testimony to help others fight their addiction. Amidst all the tragedy that has resulted from this opioid epidemic, Darren has the courage and support to share his story and inspire thousands of people in this book. Darren is a survivor!

Today, Darren doesn't just represent the biggest stars; he has become a star in his own right in the world of recovery. He speaks in schools all over the country, and he is dedicated to Turning Point, where he was awarded the Lifetime Achievement Award at their recent gala. Darren has appeared on *Dr. Oz* and other national media to share his message on recovery. Recently, he began working with the White House Commission on Combating the Opioid Crisis, where he plans to educate youth on how they can build self-worth and faith so they don't go down the same road he did.

Over the years, I have watched Darren Prince grow in his business, tackle his addiction, and now lead a life of spirituality and inspiration. I am extremely proud of the man he has become, and I am honored to be a part of Darren's family. I hope his book inspires you to overcome any battles you may be fighting and to be a light unto others.

– Earvin "Magic" Johnson

INTRODUCTION

I AM STANDING IN THE ELEVATOR NEXT TO ONE OF THE greatest boxers, one of the greatest sports icons to have ever lived. I look over to where Joe stands. At this point, he is Joe to me. Not Smokin' Joe or Heavyweight Champion of the World. Joe Frazier is one of my biggest clients and closest friends. We are in Joe's adopted hometown of Philadelphia. It is 2002, and we are on our way to meet the other most iconic Heavyweight Champion of All Time. He is the man simply known as, "The Greatest": Muhammad Ali. They have barely seen each other in 30 years. This is the biggest moment of my career. The biggest moment of my life, and I am completely loaded. I slip another pill into my mouth. I'm so good at it, no one notices.

There had never been two bigger stars than Ali and Frazier. Since the early 1970s, when their rivalry reached epic levels, Joe Frazier and Muhammad Ali had only been in the same room a couple of times. On those occasions, they had to be separated so a real fight didn't break out. The anger and resentment left in the wake of those years was far more devastating than any blow in the ring.

It was 1975, and boxing had never been bigger. The champs had already had two fights, and the "Thrilla in Manila" was the fight to end them all. Ali knew how to raise the stakes before a bout, calling Joe an "Uncle Tom" in the press and before they made it to their final fight, "The Gorilla in Manilla." Joe could never forgive Ali for that. They took all of this energy into what became a brutal trilogy of fights and the greatest rivalry in sports history. In the first bout, known as "The Fight of the Century," Joe had won, beating Ali who was just returning to the ring after being exiled for protesting the Vietnam War. In their second bout, Ali rebounded, winning by a unanimous decision in 12 rounds.

By the time they made it to Manila, their third and final fight, whatever love had existed been between the two was long gone. It was a 14-round battle between two men who could kill someone with a punch. Frazier was almost blinded by the bout, and Ali later admitted to being close to dying. They brawled for 14 rounds in 106-degree heat. Joe couldn't see by the end. Many thought it was the fight that destroyed Ali's body, if not his mind. They never spoke a kind word to one another again... until that night in 2002.

In 2001, Ali finally apologized to Frazier in a *New York Times* interview for all the things he said about him. Joe, who had once joked that he would throw Ali into the fire after he lit the 1996 Olympic torch, took the apology to heart. A year later, Harlan Werner, Ali's marketing agent and one of my closest friends and mentors, and I started trying to set up a reunion. Harlan was meant to be a part of the meeting, but with the last-minute invite he was stuck at a convention in Vegas and couldn't make it to Philadelphia in time.

"Don't worry, Darren. They'll see each other again, and I'll be there for next time," he said before the meeting. "Besides, this is history."

Joe stands calmly in the elevator, as though we're just going for a friendly stroll. We're there with his son, Marvis, and my good friend and fellow agent, Nick Cordasco, and it feels like the air has been sucked out of the elevator. Of course, that might just be the Percocet. We reach the floor of the hotel, where Ali is staying for the NBA All-Star Game.

The elevator dings, and Joe steps off. He is nearing 60 and moves slowly, like someone whose body has been beaten for decades because it has. He's still Smokin' Joe, wearing his three-piece suit and gold jewelry. He fixes his hat as we walk to Ali's door.

Ali's wife, Lonnie, answers, and she hugs Joe as though he is an old friend and not her husband's archrival. I walk in behind Joe's son and see Ali on the couch.

Joe walks over to the aging Champ, who has already been rattled by Parkinson's. I can tell he is having a bad night because he can't get up before Joe reaches him. Joe leans in and helps his old nemesis to his feet. Ali practically falls into his arms. We all stand there, riveted, watching these two giants just holding each other, waiting for one of them to break the silence.

Finally, Joe speaks.

"We don't need to fight no more, Muhammad," he says, leaning into Ali. "We got grandkids now. If we can make peace, we can show the rest of the world how to do it."

My heart is pounding in my ears, and I pull two Percocet's from my pocket and slip them in mouth. I am a witness to history, and I know I don't belong. I'm just a kid from Jersey, a special ed kid at that. For a million dollars, I can't tell you how I got into this room on this night, and I am so overwhelmed and terrified that all I can do is try to get out.

Pills are my way out. They are my parachute out of anything that scares me. As I stand in the hotel room, watching the two greatest champs to ever live holding onto each other, letting go of decades of pain and resentment, I can't stay present for it. I can't stay present for their greatness, and I hate myself all the more for it.

I am 32 years old, and all I can think is, "Who am *I* to work with *these* men?" So many people—world leaders and celebrities included—would have killed to be in my shoes in that moment, and I had no idea how I had gotten there.

But now, I'm going to tell you.

I'll tell you about Ali and Frazier; about Magic and Bird; about Evel, Rodman, and the Hulkster. I'll tell you about Pam, and Chevy, and Charlie Sheen; about all those times where I found myself watching epic moments, where I was the guy helping to make those moments happen.

At 15 years old, my love for baseball became a million-dollar baseball card business. By my late teens, I had turned my hobby into a successful memorabilia company. By the time I was 25, I had started Prince Marketing Group, where I was representing some of the biggest athletes and celebrities in the world. I had no clue how to do any of it without taking the edge off. I traveled. I took painkillers. I went to the best parties, and I believed that as long as everything looked good on the surface—as long as I had the cash, and the cars, and the girls—I would be okay.

For a decade, it worked. But then, living to use drugs became using to live. In so many ways, I had succeeded. From the outside, people thought I had it all. From the inside, I wanted to kill myself. I just didn't have the balls to do it.

On the other side of those famous names of athletes was another list: Demerol, Vicodin, Percocet, OxyContin, and every other pill I could use to escape from the life I didn't know how to live. In this book, I'll tell you about what it's like to be bottoming out when you're at the top of your game. I'll tell you how a special ed kid from New Jersey built a sports and entertainment marketing empire and then nearly lost it all—a couple of times.

Then, I'll tell you the good stuff, too. What it's like to stand in the shadow of giants. How it feels when you emerge into their light. I'll tell you what it's like when the using just doesn't work anymore, and you find another way. When you change your perspective and perceptions on everything in life. When you begin to see the positive in every negative, and you realize—even through divorce, even through your dad dying and the passing of those incredible men, like Joe and Ali and Evel Knievel—that we don't grow when times are good. We discover the best of ourselves when life gets hard.

I'll tell you about the four A's in life – Action, Accountability, Attitude Adjustment, and Acceptance – and how those simple words changed my freaking life.

I'll tell you how I finally got to the place where I could be in the room with some of the greatest men on earth—men who could leap tall buildings in a single bound—and know that I belonged there, that I had earned the privilege of being there.

I've learned to stay in the day. I've learned to be present to all of these mind-blowing moments. In that presence, I've found my spirituality. I've also learned that I don't have to hate myself anymore. In fact, I've learned to start loving myself. Even more than that, I've realized that none of these things happen alone. The friends and clients and fellowship around the world who I've met just by quitting the substances that were destroying my life have shown me that this rollercoaster is so much better when you're not alone, when you finally accept that you have belonged the whole time.

I hope you join me for the ride. It's been a wild one, and it's only just beginning...

Part One

The key to success is action,
and the essential in action is perseverance.

Sun Yat-sen

Chapter One

THE SPECIAL CREW

It was a Tuesday night when I announced my plan to my dad.

"I need to get insurance for my baseball cards," I explained to him. I was 14 years old, standing in front of him in my pajamas.

My dad looked up at me, confused.

"Insurance for what?"

For nearly eight years, I had been collecting cards. I sorted and organized them in binders, and since this was before the Internet, I had used the Current Card Price Guide to look up the market value for each card. My trick was that I didn't just collect the cards of the most recent players, guys like Don Mattingly, Darryl Strawberry, and Wade Boggs. While my friends fought over the greatest Yankee of 1982, I would grab the Mickey Mantle that no one else wanted. They might have gotten the popular cards, but I got the valuable ones.

After adding up my total collection, I realized I was sitting on a fortune. Well, a fortune to a 14-year-old.

My dad believed that every dream was a learning opportunity. He believed in instilling drive and ambition, not fantasy.

With a slight smile, he leaned back in his chair and challenged me. "It's great that they're worth all this money, but who's going to buy them?"

That's when I pulled out the newspaper clipping for a baseball card show in two weeks. I explained that I wanted to get a table, but first I would need to get insurance on my cards. I had done my research, and I realized that if I was going to bring such valuable pieces into a card show, I needed some backup in case anything got stolen.

After hearing my explanation, my father nodded, clearly impressed.

"Okay," he finally said. "How much do you need?"

"Like eight or nine," I replied.

"Fine, I'll call the insurance agent tomorrow and add $1,000 to our homeowners' policy."

"No, Dad," I interrupted. "Eight or nine thousand."

My father's eyes went wide, "How many cards do you have up there?"

I smiled. "A lot."

After my dad took out the insurance, I began preparing for the show. I put each card in its own plastic sleeve, with its information and price. I organized my display and created marketing materials for the booth. I spent every waking minute preparing for that show. My good friend and current colleague, Steve Simon, also decided to do the show with me. But while Steve thought it would be a cool way to sell a couple of cards, I went into it like I was building an empire. Steve's motive was to have fun; mine was to make a profit.

On that fateful Saturday, I got up at 5:00 in the morning. I remember being dressed and downstairs before my parents were even awake. I was headed to my first day of work as my own boss.

My dad and grandma Francis both joined me. They were impressed with how much time and effort I had put into the show and I think a bit curious as to how it would go.

I walked into the card show as though I had been waiting for that moment my entire life. In many ways, I had. I was at home from the minute I walked through the doors: the fast-paced movement of the cards, people negotiating deals, and those lines of tables and buyers and sellers. These were my people, and this was my calling.

I was born in New Jersey in 1970. It was a different time. Kids racing down the streets on their bikes, dropping them at the foot of their friend's front door. We would rush in while someone's Mom called out not to get mud on the carpet as we ran downstairs to the basement. We would throw on the dingy overhead light and quickly start ripping open the wrappers of our baseball card packs. Topps on the outside, bubble gum within, we were convinced we were about to strike gold.

Most kids didn't even really care about the cards. They were just obsessed with the gum, but I knew there was more inside. I opened each pack like a tomb raider.

I remember that excitement, the feeling of being there in the basement, looking at the players as they spread out before me. Did I get Reggie Jackson? Who might trade me for Pete Rose?

I get the same feeling today when I'm in the middle of the business deal, in the middle of the action.

My best friends would get bored quickly, not wanting to analyze the cards, shoving the gum in their mouths from the now destroyed wrapper, running back upstairs for a can of Coke and a chocolate chip cookie. I would look at the coffee table where all of those cards lay and pick up the ones I knew would be winners.

I liked picking winners because for much of my childhood I thought I was a loser. While the 1970s was great for racing down the street on your bike with your friends, it kind of sucked if you had ADD and couldn't pay attention in school. I was sent to what they called "the special crew." There were five or six of us in special education at the time, and half of them still couldn't talk by third grade. I had trouble sitting still. I had a big nose, scrawny body, and an even bigger 'fro. It wasn't hard for my smarter friends to tease me during those years.

I remember once walking out of my classroom and seeing one of the kids from the regular class. He stopped in front of me and laughed. "Hey look, it's one of the idiots!"

I looked behind me, convinced he was talking about someone else, but I was the only one there. When he realized my confusion, he laughed even harder. It took everything in me not to cry.

I was one of the lucky ones. At night, I would come home to a mother and father who loved me endlessly. My parents didn't care that I was in special ed. They knew it was just a matter of figuring out how to get me interested in school, not whether I was capable of excelling in it. I'm sure it was hard for them, dropping me off at school, knowing I was a perfectly "normal" eight-year old who just wanted to ride his bike and look at baseball cards, but they never let on that they were worried.

That same year, my family and I started family therapy, because that's just what you do when you're upper middle class and Jewish living in New Jersey.

I remember our first visit to Dr. Rhoda Gold. She asked me why I thought I was there.

I looked down at my hands as I told her, "Because I'm stupid."

Over the next 25 years, I would continue to see Dr. Gold. She watched me grow from special ed kid into the so-called Super Agent I would become.

Later, my "special crew" was blended into the big class, but we were kept in the back, separated from the rest of the kids. I began to make friends. Lots of them. I think being in special ed showed me that all you need was one thing in common with someone else to build a relationship. By the end of elementary school, I had friends in and outside of special ed.

The glue that bound us together was sports. I knew every stat, every game. I couldn't focus on a book report, but I could focus on all nine innings of the Mets playing the Dodgers.

Then I began to play baseball, joining the Little League team and finding a place for all that energy that couldn't be contained at school. In high school, I would go on to play tennis as well, but nothing could replace that early love of America's pastime. I would hear the crack of the bat and the whistle of the ball, and it drowned out the haters back at school. It was through baseball that I began to meet some of my closest friends.

My first escape was that big green field. I would stand in the outfield, waiting for a fly ball, watching as it came into view, and rushing up to catch it. I remember the feeling of the leather ball hitting my mitt, as my friends screamed in delight. It was a rush I had never felt before. I wanted to put it in a bottle like a Coca Cola and carry it with me wherever I went.

I felt normal out on that field. I felt normal in my friend's basement, crowding around our pile of cards, grabbing the ones we wanted, and fighting when we didn't get them.

The other thing that happened in New Jersey in the 1980s was that you went to camp.

Everyone did during the summer. I guess parents got tired of making chocolate chip cookies and filling the refrigerators with Coca Cola, so for eight weeks we all went away to sleep away camp, where we went swimming, made arrowheads, and learned how to fall out of a canoe.

At camp, I wasn't in the special crew. I got to be myself. I made friends, even began to talk to girls. I was 12 years old, and though I was still pretty goofy, I was one of those kids who was able to be friends with everyone: the jocks, the nerds, the special crew.

I loved being at camp, which is why it's so funny that it ended up being the place where I met my ultimate escape. One of my first nights at camp, I got a stomachache. I told the counselor, who sent me to the infirmary, a small tent with an on-staff nurse named Greta. She gave me something that tasted disgusting: Demerol.

But its effects were heavenly. Instantly, I felt like I was Superman. Every insecurity, every fear I had, was gone. I was 12 years old, and I had just gotten high for the first time.

I went back to the bunks, and I was the cool guy. I felt funny and good-looking, and I even had enough courage to go the bunk next door and flirt with the girls. It was like I was alive for the first time in my life.

The next night, I lay in my bunk bed with absolutely no stomach pain, thinking how amazing that feeling was the night before.

I turn to my counselor and said, "Man, my stomach hurts," and off I went to Greta's tent, where she gave me another dose of Demerol. It was in this twist of fate where I found my second great escape outside of sports. The next night and the next, I did the same thing, over and over and over again.

For three straight weeks, I complained of a stomachache and was given opiates in response. If they ran camps like that for adults, they'd make a fortune.

By the time my parents came to get me, I was hooked.

When my mother saw my medical report, she noticed the name Demerol and lost it on the camp counselors and nurse Greta: how could they do that to a 12-year-old? Why weren't they called? What was wrong with the camp counselor? What was wrong with the nurse?

I never went back to Greta's cabin, but I also never forgot about my three weeks of floating above the world without a care in the world.

When I was on Demerol, it was the first time I had ever felt normal in my life. It wasn't just that I was high; I was okay.

Because I was 12 and this was the eighties, no one had noticed that I was anxious or depressed. I was just the odd kid, the one who people didn't expect to succeed. The one most people didn't pay attention to.

During that week at camp, I felt like I had finally found my solution.

As you grow older, you realize how your childhood shaped you. How those fears of not being enough, or not being able to fit in, just took a huge stab at your self-confidence. I had a depleted reserve when it came to feeling good about myself. What I realized at camp, however, was that I could take something to refill that reserve.

I have always believed that in order to change anything, you have to be able to take action. It has always been my first step towards any growth or change.

A body at rest stays at rest, and a body in motion stays in motion.

We can't become successful, we can't grow, and we certainly can't recover without action. As they say, "Faith without works is dead."

From as early as the age of 12, I realized that if I wanted things to change I needed to be in action. I had to do something different.

With that discovery, I started paying more attention to all those baseball cards I was collecting. I started looking at their value, and I began to realize that I wasn't just a member of the special crew. I also had a special talent.

Every other friend of mine was already obsessed with girls, but every day I came home from school and organized my baseball card collection. This was how I wound up standing in front of my Dad that Tuesday night, informing him that it was time to insure my cards and go to my first baseball card show.

My dad, my grandma, and I set up the table alongside my friend, Steven, at the Holiday Inn in my hometown of Livingston, New Jersey. I think I must have learned how to create professional presentations because my father owned an advertising and typesetting company. My first presentation was meticulous. It was like a mini six-foot store. By the end of the day, I had made close to $1,000.

Even more than what I brought home in profits was what I brought home in trade. Over the next two years, I would become famous at those shows, not just because of my age but because I knew how to make a good deal, how to take a Butch Hobson and turn it into a Darryl Strawberry. By the end of my first year of card shows, I went to my dad again and explained that I needed an investor.

When I was five years old, my father took me fishing for the first time. Over the years, we would go fishing together almost every chance we got. I loved standing on a boat or on the dock next to my father while he taught me about some of the most important lessons in life. It was on that first trip when I learned one of the biggest.

It was a hot summer day, and no fish were biting. Finally, my father hooked a small sunfish and, like any good dad, he handed me the rod. I was so excited as I reeled in the fish with my skinny, little arms.

"Daddy," I asked, "Can we take it home to show Mommy now?"

"Yes, we can, but the fish will die if we take it home. If you throw it back, it will get bigger and grow."

"Then how will Mommy know I caught the fish?" I asked.

He laughed, "We'll tell her. Don't worry. She'll believe us."

I couldn't make the decision right away, so my dad built a small island to trap the fish but that would also keep him alive.

Finally, I removed the rock blocking the island and let the fish swim away.

My dad looked at me with pride in his eyes and said, "You did the right thing."

My father taught me that unless there was a family around that needed the fish to eat, we were catch and release fishermen. That way the fish could grow bigger and someone else could have the pleasure of catching them.

I never forgot the lesson, and I wove it into how I ran my baseball card business. I didn't hold onto the profit. I always put the money back in so I could get a bigger card. It was always about catch and release.

It was also about kindness over greed, which was why when I told my dad I needed more money in order to buy more valuable cards, he didn't just hand me the money as he easily could have done. He made me go fishing.

My uncle Joe was in finance, so he and my dad set up a meeting for me to pitch my business plan to both of them. I showed them how much money I had made in the last year, and then I showed them my inventory.

Mike Schmidt. Mickey Mantle. Sandy Koufax.

After my presentation, they went out to other stockbrokers. All together, they gave me $20,000.

From that day on, Joe and my dad became investors in my business.

I knew just as I knew that first morning walking into the Holiday Inn, that there was no way I was going to fail. I loved making the deal. I felt most alive when I was in the middle of a hustle.

Even today, decades later, I feel the exact same rush when I land a big contract for one of my clients as I did sitting across from my Uncle Joe and Dad, getting my first loan for $20,000.

By the next year, I hadn't just earned the money back; I had done so 10-fold. With the money the investors had given me, I had bought a very specific set of cards. I had met someone who was trying to sell his grandfather's entire pre-WWI tobacco card collection. These included T-205 and T-206 cards, which were known as landmark sets in the history of baseball card trading. These were distributed from 1909 through 1916 and came in the packs of chewing tobacco, which had quickly attached itself to the baseball industry. I bought the entire collection for $9,000.

I made nearly $100,000 off of that collection alone, but my uncle and dad's loan did more than help me turn a profit. Through that collection, people from all over the country began to know my name. I was advertising my business in *Sport Collectors Digest*, which was the bible of the baseball card industry. People started calling me to buy and trade. It was 1985. I was 15 years old, and I opened my first business: Baseball Card City.

I was no longer part of the special crew. I was running my own club.

But then I had to get my wisdom teeth removed. Apparently, one out of three kids who is prescribed opiates for dental surgery becomes addicted and later that year, I became one of them.

After my surgery, I came home with a bottle of pills, and I was lit. I was calling friends, feeling like I was on top of a mountain. Just like at camp, I was alive again. I felt cool and good-looking and popular and funny. All I had to do to feel that good was to swallow one little pill.

It was like I had been living my whole life without the ability to speak the same language as everyone else, and now I was suddenly fluent.

I wasn't just fluent, either. I was funny.

After the pills ran out, I went back to my Mom.

"My tooth is killing me," I complained, clutching my jaw as though it was about to fall off.

Like any loving mother, my mom didn't want to see her child in pain, so she took me back to the doctor and I got another prescription. It took only three days for me to blow through it. I loved my newfound solution to life. The only problem was that it didn't last.

Here is what I always say about my childhood. I came from two loving, amazing parents who would have done anything for me. I had a normal relationship with my sister, who went on to become one of my closet friends. I grew up privileged and happy. Even though school was tough, I had friends, many who are still in my life.

However, the minute I got high, I knew I was an addict.

I never would have called myself an addict, but the feeling I got from that Demerol and those pills was like nothing I had ever experienced before. My friends didn't have that same experience when they got their wisdom teeth out. Their minds weren't blown.

Mine most definitely was. What followed was decades of feeling like Superman, making deals, getting high, working with the biggest names on the planet. It all started with two things: baseball cards and pills.

Despite my success, despite how good I felt when I walked into a baseball card show, as soon as the rush was over, I was back to feeling like I just didn't belong.

Even as I started to get more popular (and money can definitely help with that) and girls started to pay attention to me, sending me notes to stop playing with baseball cards and come hang out, I still felt just as awkward and alone as I did when I was a member of the special crew. Nothing, and I mean nothing, could fill that big, gaping hole in me like Demerol or those pills from the dentist. Now, I had money to buy them. From the day I used up that first prescription of Vicodin for the next 20 years, I was high.

I went to baseball card shows high. I made deals high. I went to school high.

I was alive, and those pills became my answer to everything. I was a teenager in suburban New Jersey, so naturally drinking and other drugs came into play, but prescriptions were my drug of choice, my greatest love. With one simple gulp, those magical pills could make the whole world right. I was on top of the world, and it was just the beginning.

Chapter Two

PRINCE OF CARDS

BY THE TIME I WAS 16, I WAS MAKING OVER $200,000 dollars a year with baseball cards. Like I said, I had learned how to catch and release, investing a lot of the money right back into the business. That didn't mean there weren't perks, however. I was the only kid in high school with a cell phone, and in those days, cell phones came in briefcases like they had the code to a nuclear bomb. I would make and take calls during class, buying and selling cards while other kids had lunch or smoked cigarettes in the parking lot.

Selling baseball cards in the 1980s was like Instagram today. If you were at the top, everyone knew you.

Everyone knew Darren Prince.

As my collection continued to grow, my dad and I would travel all over the country, going to card shows, conventions, and major sporting events. My list of clients grew as well. I had buyers from all over the world: stockbrokers, accomplished businessmen, even some famous people. I was one of the biggest traders at any show and would get calls throughout the day and night for hard to find items, which I was always somehow pretty good at finding.

You can only imagine what that kind of success can do to your ego if you're 16, especially if only three years before kids were teasing you for being in special ed. I had gone from zero to hero in less than four years. I had an incredible string of friends and mentors to help me navigate the transition. I also had the pills.

Two years before, I met a fellow baseball card dealer, Frank, who became a lifelong friend. Frank and I advertised our collections in the same newspaper and had seen each other's baseball card ads.

"You wouldn't believe the cards I have," I told him when we first met.

He came over to my house in Livingston to check out my collection and see where we could strike a trade.

I was running my entire operation off of a ping-pong table in my parents' attic. Over the years, hundreds of thousands of dollars in cards would sit on top of that table, perfectly lined up and ordered, as though they were being sold at a convention.

I led Frank up to the attic. His jaw dropped when he saw my collection.

He laughed. "This is one hell of a place to keep your cards."

From that day forward, we became good friends, working together throughout the years. I learned early on that business was built on friendships. Frank was one of my first, and to this day, longest-running friends.

I don't know if it's because I had one of the best dads in the world, and so I was just naturally good at finding the right mentors, but throughout my entire career I have met the people in my business who were doing exactly what I wanted to do and were willing to teach me. The first of those teachers was Alan "Mr. Mint" Rosen. If you were a collector in the 1980s, you knew Mr. Mint or at least knew of him. He was famous for buying the front-page ad of *Sports Collectors Digest*, his overly tanned face and big sunglasses making him look like he was straight out of *Fear and Loathing from Las Vegas*.

He was loud and brash, and every kid walking into a baseball card show looked up to him. At that time, I had begun to find my new crew at those shows: Mark Murphy, David Greenhill, and Brian Wallos. We were the whiz kids of the baseball card scene, but Mr. Mint was the King. He was the industry's largest buyer of high-end cards. He would fly across the country just to view a collection. We would watch him spends hundreds of thousands on a card collection and then sell off the cards for a huge profit.

We all learned that value wasn't about the number on the plastic. It was about the value you created around the card. It was about the story you could sell.

I never went to school for marketing. I learned from guys like my dad and Mr. Mint.

I followed in his footsteps, creating a name for myself inside and outside of those baseball cards shows. I started employing my high school friends to help me run the business, and I started making money.

Lots of money.

My dad wasn't sure what to do with all of the money I was making. He would call the accountant up and explain that I had just made $60,000 but that I wanted to use some of it to buy more cards. He had to learn to be an accountant himself just to help me keep the business legitimate. The last thing he wanted was his now high-profile teenage son bringing the IRS to our front door.

My father believed in humility, and though he supported my entrepreneurship, the last thing he wanted was for it to go to my head.

"It's not what you say, it's what you do," he would always remind me, trying to keep me away from the fast-talking hustlers who crowded around the convention centers.

I learned to sneak money on the side, hiding $10,000 underneath my mattress so my Dad wouldn't do something responsible with it. That wasn't the only thing I was sneaking. With all of that money, not to mention access to cars, phones, and girls (even if I was a super late bloomer), the party only continued to escalate.

My friends and I were running major card deals between classes. We called ourselves legal drug dealers. I was making make tens of thousands of dollars in a weekend and could walk into a convention center with ten to twenty thousand people and be one of the most famous guys in the room. It was absolutely euphoric.

Even with all of this fame and fortune, however, I still felt completely empty inside.

I was beginning to learn (though it would be decades before I fully understood this lesson) that money and power don't mean anything if you don't mean something.

I would go to those conventions. I would have the best displays and the most gorgeous models. I would be talking and buying and selling and laughing and having the time of my life, but unless I was high I was never happy.

I wanted everyone to know that I was Darren Prince, and I had arrived, but it was all total bullshit.

On top of it all, I was still playing baseball. I wasn't a great player, but I was good enough to get into University of Bridgeport despite my less than stellar grades.

So, in the middle of building this major business, I moved to Bridgeport to start going to school. The problem was that the only things I really cared about were the business and the party. I didn't have room for anything else.

Over the next few years, my business continued to get bigger. My inventory included some of the most legendary cards ever produced.

I had a couple Honus Wagner cards, which were still considered the Holy Grail of cards. Honus was a baseball player back in the 1910s during the tobacco card days, but he was a notorious anti-smoker and he didn't want kids buying tobacco just so they could get the cards. After they produced the first run of his cards, he pulled the campaign. There were only around 35 cards known in existence, and I had one of them. I later sold the card for $80,000. Today, that card would go for over $2 million.

I had a Mickey Mantle rookie, 1952 Topps, which was in pristine condition. I had cards that ran in value from $40 to $40,000.

Along the way, Frank and I did a lot of business together and became good friends. I realized that it was building friendships with people, and not just relationships, that made the work about more than just work. It was really about the people you worked with.

It was learning from guys like Mr. Mint that I began to understand that selling baseball cards was more than just about the card. It was about the story behind the cards. You needed to market your sales, and marketing demanded that you create a story around the deal. I learned early on in my baseball card and memorabilia career that it wasn't just about the product or the talent; it was how the product or talent was pitched. The story behind the deal could double the value of whatever you were selling.

People wanted to see the action. They wanted to hear about the behind-the-scenes. When I made a business deal, I didn't do it in silence (and still don't). I made sure everyone knew how the deal was made.

In 1989, I was a freshman in college at University of Bridgeport when I attended a show called the 500 Homerun Club. This was a convention where they had every living 500 homerun club player in attendance: Mickey Mantle, Ted Williams, Willie

Mays, Hank Aaron. I was standing at my table, talking my regular game and showing off some cards, when Reggie Jackson walked up.

There was probably no bigger baseball star in the 1980s than Reggie Jackson. He was the Mike Trout of his time, and there he was at my table. Not only that, he was standing there, holding his rookie card, which I was selling. It was worth a couple hundred dollars at that time, but when Reggie asked me what I would sell it to him for, I gave him a discount. I mean, it was *his* card.

While we were talking, a reporter named Mel Antonen from *USA Today* came up to us. The next day, *USA Today* ran a front-page story about me and the other high school kids I was friends with who were all kings of the baseball card business, including my friends and my fellow traders David and Brian.

The best part about my friendship with David and Brian is that there was little competition between us. We all covered different sectors of the industry. David and Brian focused on more modern players, while I specialized in vintage cards and unopened packs. People would buy these packs at really high prices. It was like gambling on the gamble, and buyers loved it. I think because the three of us were never in competition, we really learned how to support each other.

That weekend while in Atlantic City, I decided to pick up some Baltimore Oriole team sets. At the time, Oriole Cal Ripken was one of the biggest players in the league. His brother Billy also played for the team, but for the most part he lived in his brother's shadow.

I was planning to go to Baltimore the following weekend to visit my sister in college, and to party with some friends. I figured I would unload the cards at a few different stores in the area, and that would pay for my expenses and drugs on the trip.

I drove home with the Oriole team sets and stopped by my parents' house to unload the cards and some other things before heading back to Bridgeport. The next day, my dorm was in chaos because there was a story on the news that there was a run of Billy Ripken cards where he is holding a bat that says "F*ck Face" on the base of the handle.

I woke up to people pounding on the door to my room, wanting to see if I had the card.

When I found out what had happened, the color drained from my face. I thought, "There is no way I have that card," but I had to find out.

That afternoon, I raced back from Bridgeport to Livingston and into my parents' house. My dad asked me why I wasn't in class.

I told him about the cards. Together, we began to look through the first team set before opening the rest of the boxes.

My dad never drank and certainly never got high off of anything illegal, but he loved making the deal as much as I did.

When we cracked open the first team set, we nearly passed out.

There was Billy Ripken holding the "F*ck Face" bat, and I had hundreds of them.

I had bought a hundred of these sets for $5 a piece, and now they were going for over $100.

Over the next few weeks, the price would skyrocket from there. The cards started selling for $500, $1,000, and $2,000. I had people crowded into my dorm room, and I was handling calls like it was a telethon. We had Wall Street executives driving out to University of Bridgeport just to buy the card.

I was on my way out at college, but I was leaving with a bang. That bang earned me over six figures in less than two weeks and an even bigger name in the baseball card world.

At that point, selling and using had become routine, and school was the last thing on my mind. I never really liked school anyway, and once I made it to University of Bridgeport I didn't have two parents there to make sure I went to class or did my homework. Besides, I had a business to run. I turned my dorm room into an office, employing classmates to help me sell and move cards. Once again, we looked and acted like legal drug dealers. At this point, we all ran around with pagers, getting UPS packages almost every day. Buyers would come to my dorm room to view collections.

I still played baseball. It was the only other thing I loved to do if I wasn't selling cards or doing drugs.

Even now, all of these years later when I walk onto a baseball diamond, I feel my blood pressure drop. At that time, it was probably the only place where my brain could get quiet. Otherwise, it was just flooded with sales, numbers, stats, and how much I thought I could make off a card that day.

Selling was the biggest high I had ever found. Some days it surpassed even pills.

It was my last year of college, and by that I don't mean my senior year. By the end of my freshman year, it was clear I wasn't going back. I had a 0.86 GPA, and I was far busier doing other things, like getting booked on *The Arsenio Hall Show*.

This was at the height of Arsenio. If you were going to watch late night, it was the only thing to watch. I had gotten a call from their producer, Danny Zucker, who told me they were doing a segment on successful teenagers and they wanted to have me on. I was beside myself.

I had now been featured in *USA Today* and *The New York Post*, and I was getting booked on the biggest show in the country.

I started calling all my friends to tell them the good news.

Then I called my dad.

Ever the realist, he asked me, "Did they book you or get a flight?"

"Well, no," I started to explain.

"Did you tell anybody?" he interrupted.

I stuttered, not wanting to admit how many people I called.

"Don't tell anyone. You never know what could happen."

He was 100 percent right. A week later the show called me and told me they were pulling the segment. Yet again, it was a great lesson from my father about managing my expectations. To this day, I always tell my employees and clients alike, don't celebrate when you sign the contract; celebrate when the job is done.

By that point, it was time to tell my parents that I was quitting college. I told my mom and dad that it didn't make sense for me to stay. As much as they believed in education, they agreed. I had a full-time business to run. My mom was disappointed I dropped out, but as I continued to build the business she came to understand that it was the right decision.

We had been calling the business Baseball Card City for years, but now it had become so much more than that.

I was at the center of that business, so my father suggested we call it "Prince of Cards."

My dad was really smart.

It was the perfect name. For years, it would become my name, too. People stopped calling me Darren Prince. They just would say, "Hey, the Prince of Cards is here."

I was. I had arrived. I no longer had school holding me back. I was taking on my business 24/7. I was in action.

At the same time, I was falling even deeper into addiction. I had now expanded beyond pills. I would drink, smoke pot, and use whatever other drugs were around. Perhaps worst of all and the one thing that still affects me to this day, I was abusing steroids.

It had started when I was playing baseball. I was great in the field playing first base, but I struggled at bat. I just wasn't strong or fast enough. Discovering steroids, however, changed everything.

The truth was that everyone did steroids back then. Plus, growing up as an awkward, skinny, Jewish kid, bulking up made me feel big. The steroids made me feel like no one could mess with me now.

People even started calling me "D-Bol" after the famous steroid Dianabol. It made me feel cool, like I was now the guy with the nickname.

When I graduated high school, I was 135 pounds. By the end of my first year in college, I was over 200 pounds. I used steroids for the next seven years. They nearly destroyed my life as much as the pills.

The pills and other drugs were starting to bring their own destruction. Here's the thing: it's easy to disguise a drug habit when you're in college because pretty much everyone is partying. It's even easier when you are building a million-dollar empire, and everyone around you is treating you like you're a God.

At that time, there were no consequences. I did whatever I wanted, and there was no one there to say no.

My parents just saw how successful I was becoming. They were focused on helping me stay somewhat grounded. They didn't always succeed. I was 19 years old. I was rich, and I was out of control.

I bought my first my first car, a Mitsubishi 3000GT, and had it souped up to the cost of over $70,000.

A few years later, when I was 23, I bought an Acura NSX, which cost $100,000 at that time. When my father saw it, he said, "That's a rich boy's toy, and you don't need it."

What he didn't understand was that I did need it.

I *needed* it all: the drugs, the steroids, the money, the cars, and the gambling.

At least, I thought I did.

No one knew about my addiction yet. To everyone else, I looked like I was doing great. I was definitely the most successful 19-year-old they knew, yet I still made it home to have dinner with my parents on the weekend.

What could go wrong?

With Prince of Cards, I didn't think anything could. I was beginning to expand into more memorabilia, extending beyond cards into autographed jerseys, photos, and other collectibles. I was meeting some of the biggest people in sports, and they all knew me.

I had become famous in the world of sports, and I wasn't even old enough to legally drink.

I was aiming high, and with each convention I only became bigger. The cards sold for more, I met more people, and I grew the business.

Every day was such a high. It felt like every time I threw the fish back out, it returned 10 times bigger.

I was the Prince of Cards, and no one was going to get in my way...except me.

Chapter Three

BIG GAME

MOST PEOPLE WHO MET MUHAMMAD ALI COULD TELL you about the first time they encountered the legend, but I'd like to think my story stands out.

It was 1990. I had just turned 20 years old and was visiting Arlington, Texas for the National Sports Collectors Convention. My friend Dan and I were walking out of our hotel in the morning on our way to the airport. It had been raining, and the sky was grey. We walked through the front entrance of the hotel when we saw this large, African-American man approaching. He was wearing a big, white bathrobe and strolling towards us as though he was out for a morning walk.

We were probably 30 feet away from him when we realized it was Muhammad Ali. He walked up to us and stopped. We didn't even know what to say before he pointed to his feet and said, "Look."

Suddenly, Muhammad Ali started to levitate.

I'm not kidding. Almost 30 years later, and I can remember it like it was yesterday. Dan and I stared in disbelief as Ali levitated three inches off the ground. Then, he came back down.

With a sly smile, he said, "It's the spirit." Then, he handed us Islamic pamphlets.

We were so stunned; I don't even think we were able to say how excited we were to meet him. We were speechless. He walked off nonchalantly, as if we were just a stop on along his morning stroll. We turned around to watch him leave, expecting him to possibly disappear into thin air.

We had smoked a joint that morning, and I think at first we thought we were just tripping. Finally, I asked Dan, "Did you see that?"

Dan replied, laughing, "Muhammad Ali just fucking floated."

Years later, after I started working with Ali, I found out that he loved to do magic and when he was still healthy, levitating was one of his favorite tricks. It's still right there in videos on YouTube. Muhammad Ali could actually float.

Muhammad Ali was just the first of many legendary names I would begin meeting and working with. The memorabilia game was opening up more and more doors for me. Just like with Mr. Mint, I was collecting teachers along the way.

I might not have been the coolest guy, or the best looking, or the funniest, but I began to realize that I had my own way of connecting with people. I like to think it was my dad who taught me how to treat people as equals while still offering them the humility and respect that their positions demanded.

The following year, I went to Super Bowl '92. It was the Redskins versus the Bills. I turned around to get something to eat, and I saw my buddy, Frosty. Frosty was a collector of high-end baseball cards and memorabilia. We had known each other for a couple of years at the time. He was sitting with his friend, Bill, and this outrageous looking guy, who I soon found out was Jeff Hamilton. Jeff had been the founder and Creative Director of Guess Jeans for Men. What he had become even more famous for was designing these crazy jackets for celebrities, athletes, and a high-powered West Coast crowd. Pretty much everyone has seen a Jeff Hamilton jacket, even if they're not aware of it. He would do special edition leather bomber jackets, honoring sports teams and championships.

I'll never forget meeting Jeff that night. He was like a cross between Versace and Jimi Hendrix, super tanned, dripping in jewelry. He was wearing this black leather jacket covered in rhinestones with silver and gold dragons all over it.

I went over to say hello to Frosty and introduced myself to Jeff, who quickly told me he was a big memorabilia collector. He suggested we stay in touch and said that we could trade memorabilia for jackets.

That was the beginning of a nearly 25-year friendship, which has lasted to this day. Jeff knew everyone and not just superficially. He was friends with some of the biggest celebrities in the world. From athletes to actors, everyone loved his jackets. They still do.

The money continued to roll in, and the party carried on. I was wearing these outrageous jackets, driving sports cars, and dating the hottest strippers. Since I was now finally 21, I was also hitting the best clubs. I wore gold, diamonds, and Rolexes. Basically, wherever I went I was saying, "I might have been a learning-disabled kid in special ed, but look at me now."

Despite all the partying, I still knew how to show up for work. At this point, I had been working baseball card shows for almost 10 years. I could go in, put on the show, buy the top cards, sell them for twice their initial value, and pay the rent for months.

I knew that my next step was to begin working directly with the athletes themselves. I wanted to start coordinating and selling the merchandise instead of just trading it.

Today, the sports memorabilia industry is a multi-billion-dollar business. According to *Forbes* magazine, the industry reaches 67 million people every year. Most of those transactions take place online today, but back in the early 1990s collectors would line up for hours, even days, in order to meet their favorite sports legends or try to buy the one card they had been looking for since they were 13. Cards and collectibles took on a life of their own in the late 1980s and most of the 1990s, probably up until the last eight years. They were considered 100 percent solid blue-chip investments, and in some cases, depending on the product or cards, they still are.

Collecting was in people's blood, passed down from one generation to the next. On one side of those conventions, you would see fathers and sons and mothers and daughters coming to conventions together, always looking for that next big score to add to their collections.

On the other side of those conventions were the people who made collecting possible. They were the agents who brought Reggie Jackson and Pete Rose. They were the folks who booked the talent and ensured that everyone went home richer than they came, both in dollars and memories.

I decided that I wanted to be one of those agents, booking the events and not just selling at them.

After meeting Jeff Hamilton, I knew I had found my in. He was connected to every major athlete and their agents. He knew the people I wanted to be like. I just needed to figure out my next move. If only I could stop getting arrested for long enough to figure it out.

I was 23 years old, and I had been arrested four times already that year. That's right. 1993 was the year of Darren getting busted.

The first time was dumb enough. My mechanic took my car out for a test drive while he was repairing it, and someone ran a stop sign and sideswiped the car. The mechanic got taken to the hospital, and my car was impounded. The next day, I got a call from the police that they had found a pipe with marijuana residue in my glove compartment box. I went to court, paid my fine, and quickly forgot about it. The accident wasn't my fault anyway.

Two months later, I was at the airport in Houston, Texas with one of my buddies. Our flight got delayed, so we did what anyone does while waiting for a flight—went out to the airport parking garage and smoked a joint. The Houston police didn't agree that smoking weed was an appropriate way to kill time between flights. I was arrested and booked. My friend and I both missed the flight, but I paid our fines and got us home the next day. Another ticket, another fine, another arrest quickly forgotten.

The third arrest was at an Allman Brothers Show. I'm not kidding. I don't know anyone who gets arrested at an Allman Brothers Show. It's practically a requirement for people in the audience to be high. My friend had thrown me a bag of Xanax, weed, and Ecstasy. I quickly pocketed the pills. A little while later, I pulled out a joint because again, Allman Brothers. As soon as I lit up, there were cops on me like I was in the middle of a stakeout. It didn't take long for them to find the pills.

I was taken down to the station and booked. They decided to release me and drive me back to the stadium, but everyone I knew at the concert was already long gone.

I stood there in the empty parking lot, considering my next move. I was about to call my then-girlfriend when a van pulled up. It was one of the band mates, and they asked if I needed a ride.

I got dropped off that night from someone from the Allman Brothers Band, quickly forgetting about the consequences, which had brought me there.

Unfortunately, I had a lawyer to remind me of those consequences.

They say there is a timeline to partying. First, the partying is all fun. Then, it's fun with problems. Finally, it's just problems.

I was in the "fun with problems" stage. There was so much of my life that didn't seem affected by the drugs and booze, and yet suddenly the stakes seemed to be rising.

I knew I was in trouble when I sat in the lawyer's office, and he quietly looked through all the paperwork. I was willing to buy my way out of anything, but the attorney told me it wasn't just about paying tickets anymore. My next arrest could spell jail time.

"Just stay out of trouble," he warned. "Don't do anything stupid."

It was probably less than a month later that I was with friends in South Orange, sitting in the backseat of my friend's parked car as they passed around a joint. I didn't even think anything of it. I mean, what were the chances? Plus, I was trying my best to follow my attorney's advice so I wasn't even smoking.

My heart hit the ground when I heard the first whirl of the sirens and I saw the red and blues flashing behind us.

"Are you fucking kidding me?" was all I could say.

Though I was sober at the time, that night was my fourth arrest, and I am pretty sure it was the Universe's way of saying, "Hey buddy, wake up!"

But I didn't.

One arrest is often enough for people to look at their drug habit and say, "Hey, maybe I got a problem."

By the third or fourth consecutive arrest, they are usually well on their way to rehab.

I wouldn't get sober for another 15 years. I still had a lot of hard falls ahead of me, along with a lot of amazing highs.

I was sentenced to the Alliance, an outpatient program out of St. Barnabas Hospital in Livingston, New Jersey. I went to the center, not because I thought I had a problem but because I wanted to clear my record. I had to tell my parents, but as I explained to them, it was all just a case of being at the wrong place at the wrong time.

I mean, how could I have a problem?

I had the business, the money, and the cars, and I always showed up for my responsibilities. I was just young and experiencing a streak of bad luck.

My license had been suspended with the final ticket, but as long as I completed the outpatient program, I would get it back. Then all my legal woes would be over.

I had some business in New York City, so I went in with a good friend of mine. Since I was almost done with my outpatient program, I thought it would be appropriate to celebrate with some mind eraser shots (vodka mixed with coffee liqueur). I remember chasing the shots with a combination of Xanax and Valium because nothing will erase your mind quite like that combination.

At the time, Scores was the hottest strip club in the country, and I was on the VIP list. My friend and I made the rounds, meeting girls, throwing back drinks, popping pills, and then we got in his car to drive back to New Jersey. On that drive, my friend fell asleep at the wheel.

I woke up covered in blood and glass. I needed 90 stitches in my face, but miraculously no one tested my blood alcohol level.

A couple of months later, I got my license back.

Was I finally humbled? Did I think, "Wow, looks like someone is trying to teach me something? Maybe those classes at Alliance were right?"

The answer was no.

This is the funny thing about addiction. Until you can hear the language of your disease, it's like you don't even know what it is being said to you.

In my mind, I saw all of these events as just a series of unfortunate, but totally unrelated incidents. In my denial, I could not even begin to connect the dots, let alone admit that I had a problem.

So, what did I do with 90 stitches in my face and my newly returned driver's license?

I went out and bought that $100,000 Acura NSX, the one my father called a rich boy's toy. I answered an internal problem with an external solution. I believed that as long as my outsides looked okay (minus the face laceration) my insides would be okay, too.

I had everything a 23-year old guy on this planet would ever want, but I was absolutely miserable inside.

I figured my happiness hinged on moving my business forward. It was just a matter of getting to the next level. I was bored and had reached the upper echelons of what I could do in memo-rabilia sales.

My father used to say, "The idea is one percent and carrying it through is 99 percent."

I had an idea, but just like when I asked my dad for insurance money while standing in my pajamas, it was time for me to take action again.

I called up Jeff Hamilton in 1994. We had begun to develop a friendship, and I explained to him what I wanted to do.

Jeff was friends with Harlan Werner, one of the biggest sports marketing agents in the industry. Harlan represented everyone: Muhammad Ali, Joe Namath, Sandy Koufax, and many others.

Harlan knew how to book clients, and after meeting him through Jeff, I realized he was probably even more arrogant and pompous than I was. I liked him immediately.

In 1994, I called up Harlan and told him I was ready to expand my business.

"I want to start with signings," I told Harlan.

He could have seen me as competition. He could have told me to go screw myself and hung up the phone. Instead, this pompous, arrogant agent told me everything I needed to know in order to start booking clients for memorabilia signings for my company and start phasing out of baseball cards.

It wasn't long after my 24th birthday that I booked my first signing.

You'll never guess whom I booked. That's right. Muhammad Ali.

Harlan told me everything I would need to know in order to work with the legend: how to treat him, what the atmosphere should feel like, and every detail down to the snacks and beverages that should be served. Since Ali was a strict Muslim, there was to be absolutely no alcohol.

I already knew one thing about Muhammad Ali. The man could float.

That day of my first signing felt bigger than any I had ever experienced before. Here I was, working with one of the biggest legends not just in sports but also in history.

Muhammad Ali was a fighter to the end. He fought back against oppression and segregation as a child growing up in Kentucky. He fought his way to stardom on the 1960 Olympic team and won a gold medal in Rome that summer. He turned pro soon after, challenging what people believed athletes should and shouldn't do.

Then he became Muhammad Ali, aligning himself with the Nation of Islam, demanding equality and dedicating his life to fighting injustice. He went on television and defied every convention of how a sportsman was supposed to act. He became a star. Then, in the prime of his career, he fought the United States of America, refusing to be drafted into the Vietnam War. Ali fought for his beliefs, and he fought for those who couldn't fight for themselves.

To anyone who knew him, Ali was like a God, stepping down from the mountaintop to grace us with his wisdom and his humor, but most importantly, his fighting spirit.

I stood behind Muhammad at that first signing in Boston and slipped a Percocet into my mouth.

Harlan and I created a contract where I would then move the merchandise at upcoming conventions and in advertisements. Over the years, I did a variety of signings: some for my own merchandise, some for other sellers, and the best, at the conventions where the athletes would meet with the public.

For a lot of pro athletes, those signings weren't just a place to make money; they were the one authentic way for them to connect with their fans.

People would approach their favorite athlete or celebrity, clutching a 40-year-old collectible and looking for a signature. Even more importantly, they were hoping for a chance to be face to face with their childhood hero.

What was amazing about the people who came to meet Ali was how different they all looked. They were black, white, and Latino, men and women. They flocked just to see the legend in the flesh, laughing nervously as he tried to set them at ease with a joke. Even when Parkinson's ravaged Ali's body, he still tried to make fans feel comfortable around him. He was a lion among sheep.

Ali had built his entire life around taking action. He had changed the whole world through his faith and his unwillingness to give up the fight.

As I swallowed another Percocet and nervously shook Ali's hand goodbye, I knew it was just the beginning. I was right. An endless list of Gods would follow: Koufax, Namath, Frazier, Magic, Bird, Hulk, Dennis Rodman.

That night, I got ripped. I remember hitting the local bars with some friends, celebrating our success booking Ali. I got so wasted I could barely stand up. My guys got me back to the hotel room. I had spent the day in the light of a God. By nightfall, I was once again dancing with the devil. Somehow, I was still not able to see the problem.

After I got back to New Jersey, Harlan told me that Ali liked me. I couldn't believe it. The Greatest liked Darren Prince.

"He picks up on things," Harlan explained. "He can tell who cares and who doesn't."

That's the thing. I care. Always have. I realized that was my biggest strength. I wasn't just a businessman; I was a fan, and that would serve me well with many other potential clients.

When Ali died, former President Barack Obama mourned his passing, saying, "We are grateful to God for how fortunate we are to have known him, if just for a while; for how fortunate we all are that the Greatest chose to grace our time."

Muhammad Ali graced my life, and that weekend in Boston was just the beginning.

There was a lot more grace (and devils) to come.

Action!

Part Two

ACCOUNTABILITY

"Accountability breeds response-ability."

Stephen Covey

Chapter Four

MAKING MAGIC

YOU KNOW WHEN PEOPLE CAN LOOK AT A TIME IN their life and say it was both their best and worst time? Well, that was the mid-1990s for me.

I was booking signings and officially moving out of the baseball card game and into booking memorabilia signings and selling the merchandise. Man, talk about a rush. You would get there first thing in the morning and make sure everything was ready for the athlete. You could hear people waiting outside, their excitement and anticipation rising while they waited for the star's arrival. Then, you would get the call: Ali, Magic, and Joe Frazier were on their way.

You'd head out to the private entrance of the convention center or casino and wait for the limo to arrive. Depending on where you were, it could have been raining, snowing, or the sunniest day in Los Angeles.

You'd breathe in deep, knowing the show was about to begin. It had been over 10 years since Steve Simon and I went to that first baseball card convention, and there I was, standing outside a hotel in Pomona as a white limo pulled up and Magic Johnson stepped out.

You couldn't have been a kid in the 1980s and not been obsessed with Magic Johnson. Not only was he the greatest point guard in the history of the NBA; he was Magic.

Magic Johnson accomplished virtually everything a player could dream of during his 13-year NBA career, all of which was spent with the Los Angeles Lakers. He was a member of five championship teams. He won the Most Valuable Player Award and the Finals MVP Award three times each. He was a 12-time All-Star, a nine-time member of the All-NBA First Team, and he won a gold medal with the original Dream Team at the 1992 Olympics in Barcelona.

More than any of that, he got people excited about basketball again.

Magic was always in it for the love of the game. Whether that game was business or basketball, this was a man who simply loved to be alive and gave everyone who met him—from fans to clients to friends—experiences that would last a lifetime.

The first time I watched him dip his head down and step out of the limo, I was brought right back to watching the Lakers play the Celtics in my parents' living room, jumping up and yelling as Magic scored a triple double, even though I was technically a Celtics fan.

That was the thing about Magic. It didn't matter what you thought about the Lakers, you loved Magic Johnson. How could you not?

Magic and his assistant walked with me through the private back entrance of the convention center.

I started to give Magic the rundown of how the morning would go, offering him coffee or water, making sure he was comfortable with the schedule. He listened to me with a slight smile, like a parent obliging a toddler.

"It's a great day, Darren," he replied. "It's all gonna go fine."

It might have been the Xanax, but I immediately relaxed. I had gone from Ali to Magic in less than a year. Magic was right; it was a great day.

That year—1995—was already shaping up to be a great one.

I had met Magic a few months before at the Bowe-Riddick III fight in Las Vegas.

Harlan, Ali's manager, had put me in touch with Magic's long-time representative, Lon Rosen. After the Ali signing, I reached out to Lon about booking Magic. Magic had done very few memorabilia signings and was just transitioning himself from being a full-time player and then Coach. After announcing his HIV positive status, he had also come to the forefront of HIV/ AIDS advocacy.

Magic was a player, a coach, and had quickly become a national hero in his work to destigmatize HIV.

Lon was a good businessman and saw this as a chance for Magic to meet so many of his fans who would otherwise never get that opportunity.

At the Riddick-Bowe fight, sitting ringside, I went up and talked to Magic. I told him I just booked a signing through Lon, and he seemed genuinely excited.

That was one of the best parts of the job. Sure, it was fun to watch the fans get excited to see their favorite sports hero. It was even more fun to watch that same sports hero get excited to meet his fans.

A few months later, that signing became a reality. I had no idea Magic would end up becoming one my future mentors and closest friends. I never would have anticipated that he would take me under his wing and give me all of the life-changing opportunities that he did.

Over the next year, I proved to him that could believe in me. I would show up for him 100 percent; whatever he needed, I would always be there.

I might have been falling apart on the inside, but I was accountable to everyone around me. I showed up fully prepared. I took care of my clients. I made sure they had everything they needed. I brought the same meticulousness I had used with my baseball cards to my memorabilia signings. I wanted people to expect perfection when they worked with me, and that's what I delivered.

My father used to say: "Reputation is the hardest thing to build and the easiest thing to lose. You only get one chance."

I looked at every opportunity as my one chance, and I was determined to never get it wrong.

I was building an incredible reputation. Harlan Werner and Lon Rosen now trusted me with their biggest clients, some of the most important people in the world, and I was determined to show them that their trust was well placed.

My only secret was that I was a drug addict. To protect that secret, I began to lead a double life. By day, I ran through schedules for the likes of Magic Johnson. At night, strip clubs, alcohol, drugs, and pills consumed me.

It seemed like I couldn't do anything without being high on pills. As long as I had just popped a Vicodin or Percocet, I could walk across the conference room floor like I owned it. I could be charming and funny and engage with the most famous people on the planet. It was like every day was another day at sleep away camp. As long as I had my pills, I was Superman.

Without them, I was nobody.

I would go to Scores, wearing eight ounces of gold jewelry and a Jeff Hamilton jacket. My crew and I started rolling with security. We would pull up in our own limos and be ushered into the club. We had our own tables and our own girls. We were all in our twenties, and we were having the time of our life.

Life was grand until I woke up the next morning, dry heaving into a hotel tub, not sure what had happened the night before.

Here's the thing about addiction. The night before looks different for everyone as they get drunk or high or both, but the morning after always looks the same.

Doesn't matter whether you're puking in a trash can on Skid Row or a gold toilet at Trump International. You feel total and utter defeat.

The hardest part was that I was at the top of my game, and I was only getting bigger.

A month after the first Magic signing, I went to San Francisco for a memorabilia convention. I had just gotten my first dog, whom I named Tyson. It was late at night, and I had taken Tyson outside to go pee. As I waited for Tyson to finish his business, I saw a man walking toward me in a dark suit and chiseled hat.

Apparently, if I wanted to meet a boxing legend, all I needed to do was walk around a hotel at odd hours. There, quickly approaching me, was Smokin' Joe Frazier.

You'd think at that point I wouldn't be star struck, but Smokin' Joe occupied the same special force field as Muhammad Ali for my generation.

I grew up with stories of their famous trilogy, and I knew Smokin' Joe to be the polar opposite of his rival Ali.

He was the rough Philly boxer, not known for his poetic comebacks or his political stances. Joe was absolutely in it for the love of the sport, and the sport was the only thing he loved. Whereas Ali went onto international fame and Hollywood glory, Joe owned a small boxing gym on the bad side of Philadelphia, training kids who would otherwise be slinging weed or joining gangs.

Joe was the exact opposite of Ali in his white robe. He was the black hat to Ali's tux.

And now he was standing in front of me, bending down to pet my dog. He looked up and asked, "What's his name?"

"Tyson."

"Ha," he laughed, gently shadow boxing with the dog. "You gonna kick my ass, Tyson?"

He stood up and looked me up and down, before asking, "And what do you do?"

I explained to him that I managed memorabilia signings and that I had just done one with Ali. I told him I would love to give him my card.

Accountability. There are shining opportunities in life; once-in-a-lifetime moments when we only get one chance to say the right thing, to make the right move. Sometimes we watch those moments pass right by us, thinking later, "Man, I should have…"

Other times, we dunk that basket like MJ himself.

That night, I made a triple double. I knew there was one name that would make Joe Frazier perk up, and that was his old nemesis, Muhammad Ali.

He took my card. "You need to call me," I said. "We'll make some *real* money together."

He gave a nod to Tyson and walked back inside the hotel. Two weeks later, I had signed Smokin' Joe Frazier up for our first memorabilia signing. The only caveat was that Smokin' Joe and Ali both had riders that they would never do a signing at the same place and time.

They had managed to avoid each other's path for much of the last two decades. Their rivalry was still tense from the early 1970s, when they went round for round in those three excruciating fights. I asked Harlan if the animosity between the two boxers was legitimate, knowing what showmen they both were.

"Oh yes," he explained. "Those two don't like each other. I think Joe more than Ali, but there's not much love lost on either side."

So now I had Ali, Magic, and Smokin' Joe. I was only one year into my new business, and I was already working with some of the biggest names in the world.

Then, I had an opportunity to move out of sports and into entertainment. These were the years before Comic Con would become a household name, but collectible signings weren't just for athletes. People would pay good money and wait in line for hours (even days) to see their favorite actor, or model, or singer.

Around that time, I met someone who would become a mentor and friend. In the early 1990s, Ryan Schinman was one of the youngest NFL agents working in the league. His old agency wanted to start a new division focused on memorabilia, and he got in touch with me.

We met in New York City. I remember that after the meeting, we ended up walking out of the building together.

I told him how one day I wanted to work as a marketing agent. Ryan would go on to change the talent buying industry, creating Platinum Rye Entertainment, where he represented brands across the world, connecting them with the celebrities they needed for their campaigns. At one point, Platinum Rye worked with nearly 25 percent of the Fortune 500 companies, managing their talent acquisitions, buying talent in bulk so Ryan could negotiate the best savings for his clients.

"It's fun," he shared with me about representing talent, "but unless you have a few, good, exclusive clients, you won't make any real money."

So, I started adding more clients to my roster, the first of which was Chevy Chase. At the time, Chevy had just come off a decade-long career of blockbuster hits. He was Clark Griswold. He was Fletch. He was *Caddyshack*. He was in every great movie I had watched with my friends in our basements.

I was introduced to Chevy because a friend of mine had a brother-in-law who worked as Chevy's gardener. Through him, I connected with Chevy, who had never done a memorabilia event before. The first time I met him, I had my dad with me. Within minutes, we were in stiches. Chevy was (and still is) hilarious. He was bigger than life, and he was my first taste of working with someone outside of sports.

After our first signing, I realized that he didn't have to be my only celebrity client.

Around that same time, a collector contacted me who had received a fake Pamela Anderson autograph and was trying to get in touch with her publicist. I got the publicist's number and reached out about setting up a signing. I leveraged all the names, and I got Pam. I was becoming more confident and realizing that with each new client I was only further building my brand. I was able to utilize Ali to get Magic, Magic to get Chevy, Ali to get Smokin' Joe, and now Chevy to get Pam.

About a year later, when Pam started filming the TV show *VIP*, I talked to her attorney, Henry Holmes, who put together an exclusive memorabilia contract for Pam and me.

Now, let me stop here and remind you who Pam Anderson was in 1995.

There might not have been a more gorgeous woman on the planet. Also, there probably hadn't been a woman that famous since Marilyn Monroe. Sure, there had been Farah Fawcett and Brooke Shields and Anna Nicole Smith, but no one quite at the level of Marilyn.

Pam Anderson knew how to do one thing that none of those others could: she was good at using her fame to become more famous. She knew how to build her brand, and she also really committed to her charitable endeavors.

Just a few months before, Pam's sex tape with Tommy Lee had erupted, sending her name into every bedroom across the world. She wasn't just the lifeguard from *Baywatch*, and she certainly wasn't just Tommy Lee's wife. She was the most desired woman on the planet.

Fans would wait for days to meet her, and not just male ones either. There was something about Pam that everyone loved.

Beneath her bombshell blonde looks and killer body, Pam also exuded a "girl-next-door" warmth. She was the girl we all wished lived next door.

Pam also loved her fans. I knew that, and I figured if I could offer her an environment where she could take her fame back to those grassroots, she would not only profit but also make her celebrity status immortal.

I came home early from a trip to Hawaii to organize all the merchandise for a signing we had scheduled at the Four Seasons in Beverly Hills.

Pam arrived at the suite where I was staying with a stripper I had flown in from Scores in New York. She was obsessed with meeting Pam (and kind of looked like her, too).

I was shocked to find Pam standing there alone when I answered the door. She was pregnant at the time and was as warm and kind as everyone said she would be. I, on the other hand, was totally zooted.

Whereas Chevy was a showman, Pam was actually just a sweet girl from Canada. At the time, she was pregnant with her first son with Tommy and was trying to balance her crazy work schedule and infamous relationship with Tommy with oncoming motherhood.

When I met her, it was one of those times when you realize that money and fame and being one of the most gorgeous people on earth doesn't necessarily make life easier. Pam was trying to manage a lot.

Despite my state on that first meeting, Pam and I hit it off right away. She gave me the honor of working with her and eventually gave me the opportunity to bring her projects directly.

That night, I flew back to New Jersey with the stripper. I was high as a kite and on the top of my game.

I had now added Chevy and Pam to my growing client roster, and people were beginning to take notice. I started getting calls from other potential clients, and as business heated up, I started spending more time on planes.

Here's the thing about business travel. It sounds fun when you're saying to someone, "Oh yeah, I just got back from Hawaii last night, and I'm flying to London tomorrow."

In reality, however, you've just described hell.

I was moving between so many time zones that I didn't even know whether it was morning or night. Then, I was beginning to feel the effects of my old friends: steroids.

Steroids are brutal on the body. They basically work over every organ, scrambling your hormones and leaving everything from your joints to your ligaments wrenched. Plus, all those years of lifting more than my normal weight. I was 25, but I felt like I was 50.

The worst part of steroids is what it can do to your nipples. It's okay, you can laugh. I would if it hadn't happened to me. Out of all the side effects a steroid user could potentially experience, gynecomastia (aka, bitch tits) is one of the worst. Basically, because of the hormones, fat and tissue build up in the male chest to make it look like a female breast. Awesome, huh? Worse than the tissue buildup part is the pain.

There were days where my nipples would be in such searing pain, I couldn't even wear a shirt. Eventually, I couldn't take it anymore and finally kicked the steroids, but that didn't make the pain go away.

I needed more pills. I couldn't get out of bed without a prescription bottle beside me.

My parents had begun to grow concerned. It seemed like I was always in pain, and I was only 25. I told them it was just the work and all the flying. Again, what could they say? In the last year, I had just signed more people than some agents get in a lifetime. Clearly, I was fine. I was at the top of my game, and I was aiming high.

Since I was now working with Ali and Frazier, it made sense that my next big win would be another rival client. I went to Larry Bird, Magic's former nemesis.

While Frazier and Ali's rivalry had ended in animosity, Magic and Larry's had ended in friendship. For most of the 1980s, Bird and Johnson went head to head in championship wins, MVP titles, and the honor of being America's favorite athlete.

Their differences were stark. Larry Bird was quiet and white, playing for the fastidious Boston Celtics, who represented much of the old ways of basketball, where fans stayed in their seats and clapped pleasantly from the sidelines. Magic Johnson and the Lakers were a completely different story. They had coined the term "Showtime" to start their games because you weren't just coming for basketball; you were coming for the show.

Magic was the star, cheering on teammates, embracing them with big bear hugs. Larry and Magic were both leaders but with very different styles.

The one thing they did share was a deep and mutual respect for one another, which was why when I reached out to Larry Bird's agent, Jill Leone, and told her about my work with Magic, the usually reserved Bird agreed to do a private signing.

The signing started at 5:00 in the morning at Larry's apartment in Boston because he was working with the Celtics, and he had to get over to the Garden. I'm pretty sure it was the earliest signing in history.

Magic told me before I went to Boston, "No one's paying him to talk. He's Larry Bird. You're in the presence of greatness when you're with that man."

The minute I met Larry, I understood what Magic meant. It was like the Dalia Lama had arrived. Whereas a private signing with Magic felt like a celebration, those hours with Larry were more like a meditation.

I had grown up loving the Celtics. Just being near the man who had been my childhood hero was enough to make me want to donate my profits and do it all for free.

They say do what you love, and you will never work a day in your life. I have been in this business for over 30 years, and I can honestly say I have never worked a day the entire time.

I was working with Supermen, men who had leapt over tall buildings in a single bound, actors and athletes who had changed the world forever. People don't get famous for no reason. They become famous because they reflect the best of humanity, whether it is a fantasy like Pam Anderson or a reality like the serious determination of Larry Bird.

We stand in awe of their accomplishments, yet at the same time there is a part of us that feels like we know them. When we were kids, we thought maybe, just maybe, we could someday grow up to be just like them.

As I worked with Ali and Smokin' Joe, Pam and Chevy, and Magic and Larry, I found myself in the whirlwind of their lives: their pains, and stresses, and crises. They became more than clients; they became my friends.

The only problem was that they were friends I couldn't be entirely honest with. Even if we shared our families, our childhoods, and our fears, the one thing I could never tell them about was the little secret that always lived in my pocket. I couldn't tell them about the pills that I was unable to live without.

Chapter Five

SMOKE & MIRRORS

IN 1995, THERE WAS NO BIGGER TEAM THAN THE Chicago Bulls. They were the Lakers and the Celtics from the 1980s combined. They were unbeatable, unstoppable. They were absolutely electric.

Everyone who worked in sports wanted a piece of their action.

Michael Jordan was the name of all names. He married the showmanship of Magic with the quiet leadership of Bird, was named to 10 All-NBA first teams, added nine All-Defensive first-team selections over the course of his career, and was among the greatest winners in NBA history. During the early portions of his career, Jordan had to go up against all-time great teams like the Larry Bird-led Boston Celtics and the Bad Boy Detroit Pistons. When Jordan was finally able to reach his first NBA championship in '91, he didn't look back. Jordan led the Bulls to six NBA titles and was named finals MVP all six times.

The Bulls broke every record imaginable.

As a memorabilia company, you can only imagine the amount of sales we were doing around the team.

This was where the best of times began to turn into the worst, though, at the time, I had no idea.

I had been working with a broker out of Boston who was selling Jordan memorabilia. Jordan didn't sign a lot, so his stuff was some of the most highly valued on the market. That year, I started selling signed Michael Jordan autographed items, as well as some Chicago Bull team-signed balls with signatures from all 12 players.

All of the merchandise was authenticated by an FBI forensic document expert, who was endorsed by the Bible of the Sport Collectibles Industry as one of the best.

At their height, the Bulls were bigger than life, coached by the great Phil Jackson and teamed with Michael Jordan, Scottie Pippen, and Dennis Rodman to complete the triangle offense. In the off-season before the 1995-96 season, the Bulls were in desperate need of a starting power forward. Rodman was also the best rebounder in the league. Though he had been on the Detroit Pistons during the great Chicago-Detroit rivalry in the late 80s and early 90s, he quickly settled into the red and black uniform of the Chicago Bulls. Together, Dennis, Michael, and Scottie would form one of the greatest trios in NBA history, winning the Championship title for the next three seasons with the Bulls.

Dennis Rodman came to the team on fire. They had already won three championships a few years earlier, but Dennis brought true grit to the game. When we talk about love of the game, we talk about Dennis. If he could play the game until he turned 100, he would.

It was in that year that I got to meet him. It was 1996, and I was at the NBA Finals with Jeff Hamilton. With Harlan's help, I had been trying to get Dennis for a signing because, like I said, everyone wanted a piece of the Bulls' action.

Jeff knew Dennis' agent, Dwight Manley, and had already made several jackets for him. Jeff saw an opportunity at the fifth game of the finals. The Bulls had just won on their home court. Dennis was the star of the show.

When I say Jeff Hamilton knew *everyone*, I wasn't kidding. In the middle of the mayhem, Jeff introduced me to the world's greatest rebounder, along with his agent. Dennis invited me to catch up with him later at Crazy Horse.

Crazy Horse was the best strip club in Chicago and the frequent home of many local athletes. I figured Jeff and I would go together, but he had other plans. This was another moment, just like that one outside the hotel in San Francisco with Smokin' Joe. I saw my opportunity, and I wasn't going to blow it.

I know most people see accountability as showing up for other people, but I believe first you have to be accountable to yourself. You need to be accountable to your own dreams and goals. If you're not willing to take the risk for those dreams, who else will?

So, I showed up at Crazy Horse on the craziest night of their year. I was high as a kite, having swallowed four Percocet pills. I walked up to the door of the VIP area.

George Triantafillo, Dennis' bodyguard, was at the door. I told him I was there to see Dennis Rodman.

He asked, "Who told you to come?"

"Dennis did," I confidently replied.

Dennis came out and brought me right in. I remembered thinking it was so weird. Dennis was the biggest guy in the world. This was one of the biggest nights of his career, and he came out to get the random white dude, waiting outside the velvet ropes.

I'm not sure there is a better story to capture Dennis. He is larger than life. He has long struggled with alcohol, and when he's on fire, you cannot shut him up.

But Dennis Rodman is also a great man, and anyone who is his friend can attest to the fact that he is one of the most loyal friends you will ever find.

That night was the first of many nights with Dennis. We both liked to party, so it was an easy connection. We also both liked strip clubs. From Crazy Horse to Scores, from Las Vegas to London, we travelled the world together. We had a lot of wild nights and a lot of brutal mornings. For both of us, business always came first, but the fun wasn't too far behind.

The 1996 Atlanta Olympics began two weeks later. Muhammad Ali was scheduled to light the torch. I had created an exclusive contract through Harlan to sell 1,996 limited edition signed photos from the experience.

I remember looking at the picture. Ali's body struggled from Parkinson's. I was reminded that even though these men might be mortal, their stories would last forever. Dennis, Michael, Magic, Smokin' Joe, Muhammad. They had all made history.

By now, I had become a part of the Ali family, and I began to realize that this was what made me different from a lot of the other people in my business. Lonnie and Muhammad knew my parents and sister, and I was getting to know their family as well. It wasn't just about business, particularly with guys like Ali and Smokin' Joe.

After they were gone, it was these moments that remained. The picture of Muhammad, leaning in to light the torch, shaking yet strong.

Eight days later, a bomb was detonated at that Olympics, killing one person and injuring other people, forever marring the event's memory. For me, however, that moment in history would always be about Muhammad Ali.

In those days, there were so many times when I would be somewhere—sitting ringside with Smokin' Joe in Las Vegas; in the VIP section of a strip club with Dennis; riding next to Magic Johnson through Los Angeles—and I would think I was dreaming.

They often say when you're using drugs that you're self-medicating. I think that more than anything the drugs made it possible for me to stay cool during so many of those surreal, stressful moments. Without the drugs, I didn't feel like I belonged. So many times—even at some of the best—I just wanted to run. I didn't know how to be present because I was absolutely over-whelmed by my own life.

I had what they call a case of "Imposter Syndrome." I didn't belong there; I didn't deserve to be there; and I was pretty sure someone was going to find me out.

I was going to be thrown out of the club, escorted out of the ring, dropped off on a random curb in LA. "Find your own way home, kid," someone would yell after me.

I knew it wasn't going to last. For the next year, it almost didn't.

So, remember how I told you about the Michael Jordan mem-orabilia I was selling? How I had gotten it authenticated and made some easy money off of it?

Well, there's a bit more to that story than I even knew at the time.

For the prior two years, I had run a column called "The Autograph Experience" in the baseball card magazine, *Tuff Stuff*, which was one of the bibles of the industry. I would share stories of what happened at various memorabilia signings, the behind-the-scenes for collectors and fans alike. I had learned those early lessons from people like Mr. Mint that you needed to keep your face on the front of your business. Since I had become an expert in the field, I used the column to continue marketing Prince of Cards.

This was why I wasn't surprised when the FBI called. They told me they were working on an investigation, and they needed my help.

"We're willing to pay you for your help," the agent told me over the phone. He asked if I had an attorney, and I said I would call them back.

Then I called my attorney, Marc Garfinkle.

"Don't say anything else," he advised. "And I'm coming with you whenever you speak with them."

We scheduled the meeting to take place in Chicago a few weeks later. Marc and I both planned to fly out.

The night before we left, I got a call from the broker behind the Michael Jordan memorabilia, and then I began to realize what this was all about.

"They're trying to get me on tax evasion," he lied. "They're going to try to get you to turn on me, but I swear I haven't done anything wrong."

The next day, the Feds explained that most of the Michael Jordan and Bulls memorabilia I had been selling over the last two years was fraudulent.

I explained it had all been authenticated by one of their own, an FBI forensic document expert. The FBI kept pushing. "You should have known or asked more questions." "How are you positive that he really signed all this stuff?" "Didn't you know he had a contract with Upper Deck?"

They asked me if I ever had any issues with customers wanting their money back because they doubted authentication.

I told them, "No. Look, I've never had any issues with refunds. And I know, deep in my heart, that what I am selling isn't fake. I don't sell fake product. Besides, the forensic expert I use has been advertised and praised by *Sport Collectors Digest*, and they're one of the leading voices in authentication."

That's when I saw the shit-eating grin on the agent's face.

They had tapped my phones, and they played a recording of one of my sales representatives arguing with an attorney in Hawaii about the Bulls team-signed ball. The attorney had bought the ball months before and was just then calling to question its authenticity. My rep rightly told him that it had been too long since he made the purchase.

"How do we even know if it's our product?" he asked.

I listened to the recording, hearing the exchange for the first time. My rep had never told me about it because we weren't concerned about the product.

The FBI was convinced they had me. I had just said on record that we had no issues with refunds, and there in black and white they had one of my representatives talking about a refund.

Because I was the business owner, the accountability fell to me.

They told me I was a target in the investigation and not to leave the country. I went back to New Jersey and went to work. I started sending out refund letters to everyone who bought the Jordan pieces. I issued hundreds of thousands of refunds and ended up nearly a million dollars in debt.

Before my hearing with the judge, I went to all those amazing friends and clients I had been building up over the last three years.

These were people who I stood in complete awe of, and now I had to go to them and say, "I screwed up, and I need your help."

They were the hardest calls I ever had to make.

What I discovered was that accountability is all about risk. When we're willing to be hurt, when we're willing to fail, it means we care. When we share our weaknesses alongside our strengths, we allow people to know us for both. In the process, we usually find out that our weaknesses can be our strengths.

I didn't question whether those products were fake. I had a good relationship with the memorabilia dealer in Boston. I trusted him. In this case, my trust might have been a terrible judgment call, but it was also why people like Magic Johnson, Dennis Rodman, the Ali family, and Harlan were willing to write letters of recommendation to the judge on my behalf.

Then, I had to prove to my customers that we were still selling quality stuff. I had to restore my reputation across the board.

I was facing federal criminal charges, and my business had gone into a million dollars of debt. The hardest part was that I had to ask my most valuable clients to save me from my own mistake.

I had gone from being on top of the world and not knowing how I had gotten to there to almost losing everything in one year. I was completely confused.

We've all had those highs and lows, those times in life when you look back to just one year before and can't believe how different everything looked. It's crazy how quickly everything can change.

After the judge heard the case and read the letters of recommendation, he said, "It's clear there are a lot of people who respect and care for you, but you also made a very poor choice in selling these items to your clients."

He gave me three years of probation.

My conviction was all over the newspapers and all over the collectibles industry. The Prince of Cards had just become a felon.

I was determined to make it right. I started to rebuild my business, and I decided to quit doing any illegal drugs (in my mind at that time, pills weren't illegal). I got them prescribed from a doctor. I thought that by quitting everything else I would be able to rebrand my business the right way, starting with all of my amazing clients who stood by me during that time. I realized that throughout my career, I hadn't just launched a business; I had built a family.

It was crazy that when I was doing well, I never felt like I belonged. I would have to pinch myself while having lunch with Magic or partying with Dennis. Now, I'd shown myself to these same people at my most vulnerable. By letting them see my fears, they suddenly became more human, too. We became closer friends, and Magic Johnson was at the front of that line.

It wasn't long after the sentencing that I was riding with Magic in a limo in Atlantic City.

I was telling him about the financial damage from the Michael Jordan stuff and what I was trying to do to save the business. Then, I started to cry.

Magic stopped and looked at me.

He said, "Look man, I know you're struggling right now, but God tests great men and women, and he tested me with HIV, and he's testing you right now. Darren, you're going to make lemonade out of lemons."

He thought about it for second before coming up with a plan: "How about this? At the next signing, I don't want to come through the back of the room. We're going to walk through the front of the convention center together. We're going to show these people that Darren Prince went through all this, but he still has Magic Johnson as a client."

I didn't even know what to say. Here was this man who had already done so much for me, and now he was willing to use his reputation to save mine.

I remember later calling my father and telling him about my conversation with Magic. He laughed and said, "He needs you like he needs a hole in the head, but what an amazing thing to look out for my son."

Magic Johnson wasn't the only one to look out for me. I continued working with Smokin' Joe, Muhammad Ali, Dennis, Pam, and Chevy.

I started to rebuild the business, and Magic wasn't lying. He was right there next to me.

Usually at conventions, the celebrity would enter the signing area through the back. At the next one, just like he said we would, Magic and I walked in together through the front. I felt all eyes on us, and I knew Magic was right.

Everyone was thinking, "There's Darren Prince, and Magic still believes in him."

Magic was like a guardian angel in front of me. As we came in, it was so quiet you could hear a pin drop. No one did this kind of thing, but Magic was willing to do it for me.

Everything that had happened could have been the end of my business. It could have been the end of my career, but it showed me that being accountable means making mistakes and owning up to them. I had to take ownership of my poor choices. I didn't want to see my business close; I didn't want to have to lay off my staff. I wanted to see us all succeed and to continue doing what we loved every day.

Through some pretty incredible friendships, I was able to do just that.

Chapter Six

SUPER AGENT

THROUGHOUT THE ENTIRE FRAUD CASE, I MANAGED to retain every single client.

What was perhaps even more shocking was that right in the middle of my case, I started working with another tremendous legend. The year before, I did an interview with Joe Montana for my column for a magazine called *Tuff Stuff*. I worked with his memorabilia agent, Mike Bertolini, and we developed a relationship through that interview.

About a month before my hearing, Mike and I connected about me working with Joe. Joe Montana is frequently considered the greatest quarterback in history (now closely tied with Tom Brady). As a player, he was always calm in the middle of chaos, especially in the fourth quarter. He was known as Joe Cool, king of the comeback.

In his post-career, Joe was considered one of the greatest and most respected athletes on the planet and I was thrilled to be talking with Mike about working with him. We spoke about what the signings would look like and discussed a potential contract. Then, I had to drop the bomb.

Though Mike knew I had made a big mistake with the Bulls memorabilia, I had to tell him that I was going to be facing a judge on it the next month.

"I understand if that might throw Joe off," I told Mike. "So, I just wanted to be upfront about it."

Mike didn't hesitate. "Look, Darren," he said. "We all make mistakes. Joe and I both get that. Just be honest with me and Joe, make sure it's good, clean business, that you're only selling authentic memorabilia, and we're with you."

I agreed with him.

Over the next year, no matter how scary it got, Joe and Mike stood by me. I understood why my clients who had more history with me might have been willing to stick around. Most of them had been working with me for a couple of years. They knew me to be honest and fair. They knew me to be accountable. Joe and Mike trusted me totally on instinct, and I have always remembered and been thankful to them.

I had weathered the worst year of my career, yet I still managed to have a client list that looked like a mega-Hall of Fame roster. Even with this continued success, there was something missing.

By the end of the summer, I needed a vacation. I took my dad, who had rarely gone on vacation, on a one-week fishing trip to Alaska. We had been fishing together my whole life but never outside of New Jersey. It was epic; just my father and me on a boat in the crystal waters of Alaska. It took me back to all of those years, being on the dock with my dad, and all of the lessons he had taught me.

I remembered back to when I was in high school and my first girlfriend Jodi broke up with me. I was on the phone with my friends, who were all together at another place.

They were trying to get me to come meet them.

"Leave me alone," I yelled. "I want to kill myself."

I hung up the phone, went up to the roof of my house, and walked to the edge.

It wasn't a long drop. I'm sure I wouldn't have died, but I definitely would have broken a bone or two.

The thing was I didn't really want to kill myself. I was just a broken hearted teenager who wanted the world to know.

My parents weren't home, but within minutes, my friends had all arrived. There were neighbors outside. Police cars showed up and the local fire engine. I was surrounded.

By the time my parents came home, I had gone back in the house and locked myself in the bathroom, embarrassed to have caused such a scene. My parents rushed into the house. My dad found me in the bathroom and knocked on the door.

"Darren, you okay?" he asked.

Whimpering, I replied, "No, I'm not okay. My heart is broken."

"Ohhh." I heard my dad utter a sigh of relief. "Is this your first broken heart?"

"Yes," I admitted.

With his usual candor, my dad replied, "Well, toughen up then son because it won't be your last."

I thought a lot about that moment during the FBI investigation. It was my first major heartbreak in business. There were plenty of times when I had wanted to jump off the roof, but I had remembered my dad's words. It wouldn't be my last heartbreak in business either.

The best that I could do was learn from the experience. So, I took my dad to Alaska to learn more from him. The only problem was that I was high on Vicodin the whole time.

I had stopped doing illegal drugs during my probation, and I figured that as long as I had a prescription they couldn't arrest me.

By now, I couldn't be awake without using pills. I kept them by my bedside, and as soon as I woke up I would pop a pill in my mouth. Taking pills was as natural as breathing. I didn't even think about it.

My routine never faltered. Vacation with my dad was no different.

My dad knew me like no one else on the planet, which was why hiding my addiction from him was so heartbreaking. Still, he could tell that something else was bothering me.

"What's your next move?" my father asked one day while we were reeling in trout and salmon.

As much as I had loved what the memorabilia industry had given me—the people and opportunities it had brought into my life—I was also ready for the next challenge.

Hesitantly, I told my father, "I want to be an agent."

"So be an agent," my father replied, sending his line back out into the stream.

"Yeah, it's not that simple, Dad. I don't have a law degree. I don't even have a college degree."

My dad put down his rod.

"Darren, you have something way more important than a degree. You have relationships. Do you know how many people would kill to work with the people you work with? It's who you know, not what you know, in life. It's the relationships that will give you the leverage you need to be an agent. Not a law degree."

My dad always knew the right thing to say. I often think it was my parents who stood between me and all the other really horrible consequences of addiction I could have experienced like jails, institution, or death. I had so much respect for both of them; there was no way I could break their hearts that way. Of course, if they knew what was really going on, their hearts would have been broken all the same.

"Listen," my dad advised. "Why don't you talk to Magic about it? If he supported you through last year's mess, I'm sure he'll be willing to support you in this."

Two weeks later, I was in Detroit with Magic at a public signing I had booked for him. He flew in by himself and invited me to his hotel room to catch up before the signing.

It was almost fate. Magic rarely came in alone, so I never had a one-on-one opportunity with him before. I told him that I was interested in representing my clients beyond signings. I wanted to find them marketing opportunities, commercials, and keynote speeches. I wanted to be able to negotiate their intellectual property and licensing deals. It was in line with the work I had already begun to do for most of them, but I realized that in being a full-service agent I could help them not only continue to profit from their platforms but also further cement their legacy. Magic listened carefully as I told him what I wanted to do and why I was also worried about doing it.

"I know I don't have a law degree, but I also know it's what I love to do. It's what I was born to do."

"So, who are you thinking about having as your first client?" Magic asked.

I couldn't help but hesitate before I admitted, "You."

Magic laughed lightly and then shocked me.

"Alright. I'll give you two years, and if you don't use my name to knock down every door, window, and wall to bring in every celebrity name that you can, I'll have to fire you because it's not about how successful I become; it's about how successful you become and everyone else around me."

That was it; I officially started Prince Marketing Group.

Magic asked me if I had an entertainment attorney, and I told him not yet.

"Alright. Well, get yourself a good one, and then have them get in touch, and we'll figure out our deal."

I couldn't believe this was happening. Within the next month, I hired one of the best attorneys in town, and we structured our first representation deal with Magic. I found one of the best publicists in New York, hiring Andy Warhol's former publicist, R. Couri Hay.

The week after Magic and I signed the deal, there was a piece on "Page Six" of *The New York Post* (the TMZ of its time), which read, "Super Agent Darren Prince signs Magic Johnson."

I had not only become an agent. I was already a Super Agent.

My dad was quick to bring me back to Planet Earth. "They're not calling you that because you're special. They're calling you that because Magic is."

It was a good reminder that being an agent was not about me. It was always about the client. My job in the media was to always be protecting and projecting my client's interests. As I had learned from Mr. Mint so many years ago, it was also about offering the media the story behind the story.

I had been pitching the media already for a number of years, starting with Prince of Cards. Prince Marketing Group was an entirely different beast. I started running full-page ads (just like Mr. Mint) in *Robb Report* and *du Pont Registry*. There were times when those ads nearly bankrupted my company, but we became known. Everywhere I went, people had heard of Prince Marketing Group. I was well-known by people I had never met.

My job now was to be a part of the media; to help generate positive press for my clients and promote their latest projects; and to make sure they stayed in the popular culture, even as their careers shifted. That was what I became known for. If you needed to keep your platform alive, you came to Darren Prince. I was always able to get the piece placed and the action noticed.

I was accountable to my clients in ways I never had been before. Prior to Prince Marketing Group (PMG), I was just the signings guy. Now, I was the 24/7 guy. I was the first phone call, and I couldn't have found a better position for myself.

I ran Prince of Cards for eight years, but I have been running PMG for 12, with no sign of slowing down.

My dad was right. In becoming an agent, it wasn't about a degree. It was about relationships, and I knew how to manage relationships. I had finally found my calling.

Right out of the gate, I started making lucrative deals for Magic. I wanted to position myself in the agency game with the same notoriety and passion I was known for with Prince of Cards. We started booking keynote speeches, licensing opportunities, and satellite media tours (SMTs). The more I began to build relationships with the established advertising and creative agencies, the more I was able to negotiate for my client.

Through it all, Magic became the greatest professional mentor money couldn't buy. Here's the thing about Magic: he is the talent, the management, the legal, the publicity, and the advertising all in one. I was a sponge to his advice. I absolutely zoned in on everything he had to say. From negotiating licensing to royalties to percentages, he knew how to structure a deal like no one else.

With Magic, it was simple. You did things the way he liked them to be done, and he would overdeliver for you every time. People wanted to work with him, again and again and again. I learned to pay attention to every single detail. I would manage everything from the car service to the concierge to the view from the room where we would be hosting a meeting. From the beginning, I realized that the more I was accountable for, the more experience I would gain. Plus, if something went wrong I would rather the mistake fell on me. At least, I could figure out how to resolve it for the future.

I feel like today, everyone lives to cover their ass. It's all about making sure you don't take the blame. I don't know if it was because of the fraud deal, but I had learned that in fessing up to my mistakes I not only learned from them but also showed the people around me that I knew how to work through adversity. There will always be adversity, and I had learned my lesson.

There was no better client for me to cut my teeth on than Magic Johnson. To this day, I am aware of how lucky I was that he agreed to be my mentor. Magic makes everyone in the room feel like they're the most important person in the world. He has utter faith in the people he chooses to work for him, and he brings out the best in all of them. He knows the strong points in each person, and I believe he saw in me someone who would always be able and willing to vet the deals coming his way.

Again, my goal was to protect and project my client's interests and I learned how to do that from Magic.

Magic wasn't my only mentor. I started repping Pam Anderson as well. Since it would have been a conflict of interest for me to negotiate a contract with myself, I sold off my exclusive signing contracts for her and Magic. Then, in a final farewell gesture, I sold Prince of Cards.

I couldn't have made the transition without the help of Harlan Werner and Pam's lawyer, Henry Holmes. I learned from some of the biggest names in the business. If only I could do the same thing in my personal life.

I was nearing 30 and had been single for most of my life. Sure, there were girlfriends and strippers, girls who would come and go, but no one serious. Pam and I would talk about me finding one good, solid girl in my life, but I was too busy just trying to make it through the day.

In 1998, I was released from probation. I was tempted to return to my old partying ways, but I knew that I needed to be on my A-game. For the next 10 years, my abstinence from illegal drugs became my big "But I."

"But I" don't have a drug problem. "But I" quit doing drugs. "But I" can't be an addict.

At the same time, I was beginning to experience another consequence of my steroid use. In addition to a case of Gyno (or Bitch Tits), I was also experiencing horrific sciatica. Sitting on planes multiple times of the week didn't help the problem.

I was in pain all the time and started to receive epidural needle injections. With those injections came more prescriptions.

I still couldn't meet with a client or negotiate a deal without pills. They gave me my superpowers, offering me the confidence I needed to broker the aggressive deals I was making for my clients. I figured that since I had gotten rid of the illegal drugs I could hide my addiction in a prescription bottle, and no one would know.

Then finally, I had to confront the condition that had been torturing me for nearly three years. Three times, I had surgery to try to fix the gynecomastia. It had gotten to the point where I was in excruciating pain every day. The third time, when the doctor went to prescribe me more pain meds, my Mom said, "You're not getting anything. That's enough."

Little did she know I practically had a whole pharmacy at home.

Despite the pain and the pills, professionally I was unstoppable. There was no longer a middleman between my clients and myself. Everyone called me directly: Magic, Pam, Chevy, Smokin' Joe, Dennis, and others. My friends couldn't believe it when we would be out and I would need to step away to talk to Magic or Pam or Smokin' Joe. At times, I couldn't believe it myself.

I remember reaching out to Henry Holmes, Pam's attorney, and asking him about Hulk Hogan, who was larger than life at that time (and still is). Henry also represented Hulk, and I was hoping he might connect us. Hulk didn't want to do anything. In conjunction with the WWF (now WWE) and Vince

McMahon, Hulk preferred to manage his own marketing and licensing opportunities. Still, I told Henry to let me know if Hulk ever changed his mind.

I realized that I had a special talent when it came to managing special talent. I was able to see people as being the kings of any room and the biggest of stars. Here's the thing: everyone stands in awe of athletes. Athletes might want to act or sing or play music, but all celebrities want to be athletes. They are the only high-profile profession where there isn't a do-over. You can cover something up on stage. You can get another take. Athletes have to perform live every day. Everyone wants their picture with a world-famous athlete, including every other world-famous person in the room.

I had the privilege not only to attend a star-studded events but to walk in with the one person everyone in the room wanted to meet. Thanks to my in-home pharmacy, I had learned how to negotiate the terrain.

I remember being in Los Angeles a few years later with one of my good friends, David Deutsch. We had known each other since childhood. We were partying at the Mondrian Hotel, and he saw Kobe Bryant talking on the phone over my shoulder.

He was like, "Oh no."

I was confused until he pointed to Kobe. He laughed. "I know what you'll be doing next."

Without any hesitation, I walked up to Kobe Bryant at the height of his Lakers career and greeted him. Kobe got off the phone, all smiles, and grabbed me in a big bear hug. It was like we'd known each other forever though we had only met each other years before when we did a signing together.

I headed back over to David, and he was still laughing.

"What?" I asked.

"Dude, it's just like you go into Super Agent mode, and no one can stop you. You just do it in this really cool demeanor."

I accepted the compliment, but I knew this was the real fraud.

It wasn't me who was the Super Agent; it was the addict.

After coming off of probation, I was landing clients left and right and brokering deals with new and bigger partners. In 1998, eBay launched. At the time, they were just another startup, but when they approached me to have Magic speak at their launch event at a collectibles convention in Hawaii I thought he was the perfect person to discuss the future of selling collectibles online. What attracted Magic to the event was that it was a benefit dinner for the Special Olympics.

There I was back in the memorabilia business, but I wasn't selling cards, or booking signings; I was managing the talent.

PMG was already making a name for itself, but I remember knowing that this was the event that was going to show who we really were by bringing in Magic. When I walked into that room with him, I felt a whole new level of respect.

Magic and I had gone over his speech, which included everyone he needed to thank, including the people from eBay. At the end of the list, I added my name.

As the speech began, I got up from the table. I had taken a few painkillers that evening and had already followed them with a couple of drinks. One of my friends, Amo, who was there to assist with security, saw me. He knew I was zooted and asked, "Where are you going?"

I could tell the speech was about to begin, and I knew Magic would say something about me. I remember telling myself that I needed to stay seated at the table, but I just couldn't take the spotlight. I told Amo I was headed to the bathroom and then walked to the back of the room towards the bar. I stood there, ordering my drink as I heard Magic mention my name from the stage.

"And my man, Darren Prince," Magic clearly was looking for me at the table. "He books me all the time at these great events. We have become good friends, and I really appreciate that."

"Where is he?" he then asked, looking at the table where I should have been sitting.

Someone, probably Amo, said I had gone to the bathroom.

Talk about not feeling worthy. Here was a moment I should have seized, but I couldn't accept the accolades. It should have been my big opportunity to show everyone how I had successfully transitioned into a marketing agent, but I didn't feel I deserved it. I just couldn't show up for myself.

Magic wasn't easily ruffled, but even I could hear the confusion in his voice. Here I had made this major deal to book him for this speech, connecting him to eBay, returning to my old colleagues and stomping grounds, and I left for his speech?

I threw back the drink, standing in the dark part of the room, knowing that I had failed during one of my biggest successes.

I had just turned what had started out as the greatest night of my life into one of the worst.

Part Three

ACCEPTANCE

"The Serenity Prayer teaches us to accept things but nowhere does it tell us we need to like what we're accepting."

Stephen Della Valle

Chapter Seven

FLYING HIGH

THERE IS A DARK SIDE TO DECADENCE. IN 1999, I was just beginning to discover it. Let me paint a picture of what it looked like from the outside:

I had just officially launched Prince Marketing Group (PMG) at a star-studded event in Atlanta, Georgia. Everyone was there: Magic, Pam, Joe Frazier, and Joe Montana. The place was packed with celebrities. The famous ringside announcer, Michael "Let's Get Ready to Rumble" Buffer, introduced me before I gave my speech. The place was filled with models and celebrities, and if you walked into the party you would have thought I was on top of the world.

They say there are two times in life when everyone you know will gather to celebrate your life: when you get married, and when you die. Since I was still a while away from a wedding, the opening of PMG was like my wedding and funeral combined. Everyone who knew and loved me, and everyone I knew and loved was there—friends, family, clients—yet all I wanted to do was leave.

Good or bad, I just didn't know how to accept life. If things weren't going my way, I thought I was the victim. If things were amazing, I knew I didn't deserve them. I could never just enjoy the moment or walk through the pain. The only thing I knew how to do was pop a pill and escape.

A couple of months later, I went to the Tyson-Botha fight in Vegas. I was there with Pamela Anderson, her *VIP* co-star, Natalie Raitano, and good friend, Chuck Zito. I had arranged ringside seats through one of my contacts at MGM. We walked the red carpet through the tunnel and emerged into the roar of lights and applause that was the stadium. The place was packed, and Pam was worried about getting crushed. She grabbed my hand as I walked her onto the arena floor. The crowds were going wild, and I was escorting one of the baddest women in the world. I could feel the entire stadium watching us. While that might sound thrilling if you were in one of those seats, all I could do was think about the moment when Pam might drop my hand so I could pop another Percocet into my mouth. On our way to the ringside seats, Magic stopped to give us both a hug. I could tell he was proud of the progress I had made with the company and of the growth and the moves I was making.

Muhammad Ali and his wife, Lonnie, were there. I wanted to introduce them to Pam, but the place was too packed to get them close.

The evening was thrilling and exciting and totally overwhelming. By the end of the night, I ended up at a strip club with Pam and some of her friends, getting a lap dance next to one of the most famous women in the world (talk about a bucket list item).

My anxiety was skyrocketing. I mentioned earlier that I had continued to see the therapist my family introduced me to when I was eight. I remembered going to her that year and telling her about my anxiety.

She offered me a sad smile and said, "Darren, what I want for you is to walk into any room without a star or a celebrity and not on any drugs or pills and know that you were meant to be there. That you are a well respected, accomplished person who doesn't need the girls, or expensive diamond Rolex watches, or flamboyant jackets to have purpose. To feel good about who you are."

At that point, it didn't seem possible to feel good without all of those things. Even with them, I felt terrible unless I had the pills.

Like most addicts and alcoholics, I grew up feeling like everyone else had a handbook to life that I never got. I know for sure that no one gave me a handbook on how to manage the kind of life I had created. For all of Magic's amazing advice, you either have the confidence to shoulder the burden of fame or you don't. Instead of confidence, I had Percocet, Vicodin, and Oxycontin. They helped me to negotiate every social situation, every business deal, every event where I had to play the "big guy" when I still felt like that scrawny kid in third grade going to the special ed class.

As long as I had my pills, I could accept any situation. I had the playbook. Even more than that, I was rigging the game. I was

Super Agent Darren Prince, the life of the party, the guy no one could keep down.

Plus, I was doing it practically on my own. Then, everything started to change.

It was around this same time that I got to know one of the core guys who would go on to form my crew and my business. I was driving down to Philadelphia with my assistant, Christine, to meet with Joe Frazier. Christine's brother, Nick, was a big Joe Frazier fan and was joining us so he could meet the legend. He hadn't said a word the whole trip until Christine mentioned that I loved Scores, the famed New York City strip club.

That broke the ice, and by the time we made it to Philadelphia, Nick and I had become good friends. In the past 20 years, Nick—or "Nicky C." as he is known—has become like a brother to me. He started out in title insurance before getting into the memo-rabilia game, and now he works with PMG and all of our celeb-rities. Not only has he brought on Charlie Sheen as a client, but he also has great relationships with Sylvester Stallone and other celebrities he signed after moving to Beverly Hills.

When my life started to fall apart, Nicky C. was one of people who was the most shocked. He had partied by my side for years and never thought I had a problem. During those years, it was all about getting bottles comped at the hottest clubs. He had no idea that the cocky hustler getting bottles comped at the hottest clubs was a total fraud.

In the late 90s, New York City was *the* place to be. It was before 9/11, when everyone was making money. We were in the middle of the tech boom, and New York drew people from all over the world to party. The Hamptons had just exploded. Summers in the Hamptons were filled with beach house ragers while winters were a mix of Vegas, LA, and the hottest clubs in town—Tao, Lavo, Marquee.

The biggest club kings—Noah Tepperberg, Jason Strauss, Joey Morrissey, and John B, as well as publishing mogul, Jason Binn—had become my boys. I would go to all of Jason Binn's red-carpet events and launch parties. It got to the point where I was in "Page Six" almost every week, hitting the town with different celebrity clients. I had built my brand. If you wanted to be known in the New York scene, you worked with Darren Prince and PMG.

My guys and I would go out at night like we were the talent ourselves. We had security with us because it just made it easier. Our detail—Darek Robinson, Dennis Mitchell, and Marko Joyner—protected us from ourselves. They were more than bodyguards; they were guardian angels. Plus, when you've got security around you, you can walk right up to any velvet rope in the world and be let right in. From there, we would order from whatever menu of debauchery was in front of us. Again, I had quit hard drugs to maintain my business, but that didn't keep me from getting lit every night I was out on the scene.

I was Super Agent Darren Prince, and I was unstoppable.

I was living big: the women, the press, and the attention. If you're secure in yourself, you can maybe (and that's a big maybe) make it through those waters without losing your shit, but I couldn't do it. It went straight to my head.

It was around this time when I got my second and most embarrassing tattoo. I got my first when I was high on weed in my early twenties. I had Prince of Cards tattooed on the top of my left leg. Now, almost 10 years later, I found myself in West Hollywood with Nicky C. I had just popped a couple of Percs and was flying high. I decided to have the words Super Agent tattooed on my other leg, Superman symbol and all.

I really believed that I was the super one, which is probably why I always felt like such a fraud. I wasn't the super one. It was my clients who had achieved the real feats. My job was just to make their lives easier. Today, I don't think any agent in the world should feel responsible for a client's career. The client is the one performing and putting in the work and practice to become a legend. They make us. We don't make them.

It doesn't matter whether you're negotiating a $3 million contract or a $30 million one. The client is the one behind those dollar signs. We are just the middlemen.

For all of my bravado, I knew that wasn't who I was pretending to be. My parents raised me to be kind to everyone. My dad taught me to throw the fish back. I came from a family who knew what was important in life. Even still, for so many years my priorities seemed to revolve around money, pills, women, and my clients.

I didn't have room for anything else.

Not for my own health, and not even for a personal life.

At least, I didn't think I did.

Then, I started working with Dennis Rodman.

During 1996 and 1997, I worked with Dennis and his former agent on a couple of signings. After those couple of years, however, we fell out of touch. Then, one night in 1999 Dennis left me a voicemail. I could tell he had been drinking, but he told me that Los Angeles Lakers owner, Dr. Jerry Buss, had come to his restaurant and told Dennis he wanted to sign him to the Lakers. Dennis told me, "You need to call me, bro. I need you as my agent ASAP."

Let's stop there. I was a marketing agent, but I wasn't a player's agent. In order to represent someone in the NBA, you needed to be certified by the league to negotiate basketball contracts. Those were the people with law degrees.

Even still, from everything you have learned about me so far you would think I would have jumped at the chance to work with Dennis and Dr. Buss.

For over 30 years, Dr. Jerry Buss was the godfather of basketball. Since he purchased the Lakers in 1979, Dr. Buss oversaw an era of incredible success in LA. Under his ownership, the Lakers won 10 NBA championships. More than that, Dr. Buss turned basketball into the biggest show on earth. The Forum Club was the place to see and be seen, and he charged top dollar for courtside seats, making it the hottest ticket in town. He partied with celebrities, dated supermodels, and played high-stakes poker. Perhaps even more important, he developed deep, long-lasting friendships with his players. Helping to mentor the likes of Magic Johnson and Kobe Bryant, not just as players but also as businessmen in charge of their own brands.

Jerry's daughter, Jeanie Buss, has followed in his footsteps. I'm privileged to call her a friend and have been amazed to watch her take over the team.

Dr. Buss wanted Dennis on the Lakers, but Dennis needed an agent to negotiate the deal.

I didn't call him back right away. It was a crazy weekend, and I was already overwhelmed with my current clients, so it took me until the next week when I finally called up Dennis' former agent, Dwight Manley. Dwight told me to connect with Dennis' sister, Deborah, who was helping him to manage everything during that time. I left her a message but didn't hear back.

A few days later, it was announced that Dennis was joining the Lakers, but within months the new acquisition began to fall apart. It was a rough time in the Lakers' history. In 1999, the Lakers were divided between two star players, Kobe Bryant and Shaquille O'Neal.

The hard part was that Dennis had started on the team with nine undefeated wins. He was doing so great for the Lakers. *Sports Illustrated* even did a cover story with the headline, "Rodman to the Rescue."

In the locker room, it was a different story. Dennis struggled with the immaturity of a young Kobe and a young Shaq.

Since 1996, both players had dominated the Lakers franchise, known as much for their star power as for their animosity on and off the court. O'Neal was already a seasoned player at that point; Bryant had just graduated high school. O'Neal took Bryant's confidence to be arrogance and immediately distanced himself from the aloof 18-year old. From the get go, this set up a conflict with Dr. Buss, who saw Bryant as the future of his franchise. He expected mentorship from O'Neal, not competition.

Dennis said he needed a break for a day or two, and Dr. Buss took him to Vegas for some high-stakes gambling. Dr. Buss told him, "If you can just sit tight and wait to the end of the year, I'm bringing in Phil Jackson. I'm going to get him no matter what."

And he did.

Over the next eight years, O'Neal and Bryant would win three NBA championships under Phil Jackson. They would never make peace, and the year 1999 was the height of their in-team rivalry. Dropping someone like Dennis Rodman into the middle of chaos like that was bound for disaster. He immediately began to complain that the locker room was like being back in high school, as the conflict between the two star players had divided the entire team.

All he had to do was stay around for another month and a half and he would have been on another super-championship team, but by the time Dennis returned from the Vegas trip it was too late. Dennis played 23 games with the Lakers that season before he was released.

I have a lot of what-ifs from that time. What if I had represented Dennis for the contract? Would I have been able to help him through that rough patch? Could I have helped him to extend his Lakers career?

What if I was sober and clear-headed during those big years? How much bigger could Dennis' career, his legacy, and PMG have been?

I remember feeling like I couldn't keep up. It wasn't just the pills. I was managing too much with very little help, and my business was definitely taking hits because of it.

At one point, I had spent so much on marketing and advertising I nearly bankrupted the company. Then, the IRS came calling.

Basically, I was high on pills, and I wasn't paying attention. In 1997, I started getting IRS lien notices for PMG. My Dad did what he could to help me, but one day I woke up to a call from the bank. They said that $12,000 had been taken out of my personal account from the IRS. Nearly 10 checks bounced as a result. I was already behind on my car payment and mortgage, and now I was totally tapped out. I went to the bank, but they said there was nothing they could do.

I told my old friend Frank Basile about it in the morning. When I came home that afternoon and opened my desk drawer, there was a check for $12,000 inside from Frank. He left a note that said, "Take a deep breath, Prince. You will get through this. Pay me back when you can."

I needed help, and my friends and family were doing their best to help me.

I just didn't know how to help myself.

On top of it all, I was living in excruciating pain.

The steroids and heavy lifting had wreaked havoc on my body. I suffered from sciatica almost daily. It became an easy excuse for my prescriptions. I was 29 years old and couldn't get out of bed until the painkillers took over. Every day, my disease told me that I needed the pills to work; I needed the pills to wake up; I needed the pills to live.

I didn't even have to go to the streets to get them. I had access to doctors who would give me whatever I wanted, whenever I wanted. In those days, no one was paying attention. I would give doctors memorabilia or let them talk to my clients and meet them in person, and they would write whatever prescription I wanted with endless refills. I would tell myself that since it was legal, what I was doing was perfectly normal.

How could I be an addict? I was simply a patient.

I used a similar excuse for my partying. I didn't go to the clubs because I wanted to. I went because I had to. Whether I was there with clients or not, being on the scene was part of my business. I had to be out. I had to be in "Page Six" and in all of the gossip columns. I wasn't an addict or an alcoholic. I was a legend in my own mind. Life, however, had a way of trying to show me that I might be both.

It was then that I experienced complete and utter demoralization. It was 1999. I was in LA with Nicky C., partying at Asia de Cuba at the Mondrian. If Tao was the place to be in New York in the late 90s and early 2000s, then the Mondrian was the place to be in LA. Sky Bar and Asia de Cuba was where everyone went. You had dinner, you got some drinks, you met some girls, and you took them upstairs. By morning, you would meet back up with your guys for breakfast and laughs about the night before.

That's exactly what Nicky C. and I planned to do, except the next morning I wasn't laughing. At dinner, I had popped a couple of Percocet's. I remember feeling pretty woozy by the time the bill came. Nicky C. had met a girl, and they left the hotel to go out. That was the last thing I remember.

The next thing I knew I was back in my own room on my bed. I was lying on my stomach with my pants around my ankles. I jumped up, feeling immediately like something had happened to me. I looked around the room, and it had been ransacked. My wallet was gone. Nicky C. had done a signing with Pam Anderson the day before for a memorabilia company, and all those photos were gone too. On the bed lay a half-eaten cheese platter.

I had no idea what happened.

A few days later, Nicky C. got a call from a guy who called himself Dr. Bomb. He had gotten us mixed up and was trying to blackmail Nick, telling him that he had his wallet and talking about his genitals. We laughed about it after. Nicky joked, "Dr. Bomb probed your bunghole while eating a cheese platter."

The truth was that I felt sick and embarrassed.

I was such a fucking mess, but I was too embarrassed to report it to the police. At this point, I was something of a public figure and didn't want it getting out there. It's a story I hear from a lot of guys—and sadly, way too many women—who have gotten sober.

We have so many stories of how our drinking and using took us to horrible, demoralizing places. We may have learned to laugh about it, but that didn't make it any easier the next morning, looking at our reflection in the mirror, wondering what the hell just happened.

Later, we found out that the LAPD was investigating the guy for pedophilia and ended up busting him on other charges. Who knows what happened that night, but I chalked it up to bad timing. I refused to see that it might have been a result of my addictions. Besides, I had more important things on my plate.

In 2000, I got another call from Dennis Rodman. This was the call that would change our lives forever. After his short stint on the Lakers, Dennis wanted to rejoin the NBA again. I knew his return wouldn't happen without help. He needed someone to guide him back, and I knew exactly who to call.

"Is he serious?" Magic asked me.

"I'm pretty sure," I told him. "I think he was really disappointed that the Lakers didn't work out. He wants to find the right team. He just wants to play."

Magic understood what it was like to retire and then return. He knew it wasn't easy. He also knew how hard it was for a person to stay away from what they loved most in the world, what they grew up knowing they were born to do.

Retiring is probably the hardest moment for an athlete. People train their whole lives to do this amazing but incredibly specialized job. Different from most people, athletes die twice: once when they retire and then later, when they really die. They give up everything to perform, and if they succeed they become immortalized. Then, their careers end. They're still stars but they are fading, and they will do what they have to do to stay in the spotlight.

By the nature of the game, they don't have much of a shelf life on the field or on the court. Only recently have we seen longer careers from players like Tom Brady or Kobe Bryant. Athletes like Dennis and Magic get 10 plus years of their sport, and then what?

Dennis had been running a restaurant in Newport Beach, which had become a second home for him. However, I quickly found out that the restaurant was a weight around his neck. Dennis was hiding out in the restaurant, which was filled with hangers-on and the type of people who would drink with him and suck him dry. As long as he owned that place, getting him back into professional ball was going to be hard.

I wanted to bring Dennis to Magic's office, but Magic suggested that we drive down to his restaurant.

"Everyone there should see us coming to him," he said. "We need to remind Dennis what a badass he is and show all those freeloaders who they're messing with."

As we approached the restaurant, I could see Dennis pacing around inside. It was clear that he was nervous as we sat down to talk. This was the first time I met Dennis' girlfriend and later wife, Michelle. Michelle and Dennis ended up staying together for 12 years and had two beautiful children, DJ and Trinity, who I now consider to be like a niece and nephew.

I could tell that Michelle was a grounding force in Dennis' life, and she was genuinely looking out for him. I hoped that between Magic and Michelle, we might be able to guide Dennis to his greatest rebound yet.

Magic offered Dennis the chance to train with some of the younger Lakers players at UCLA.

"You can get back in shape, get competitive," Magic explained.

We talked about an upcoming charity basketball game in the Hamptons that PMG was coordinating, and Dennis agreed to play.

"Also," Magic added. "I'm opening up a new 24-Hour Fitness in LA tomorrow. Maybe you want to come help me and get out of Newport. You got to remember who you are, man."

As Magic spoke, I could tell that Dennis was beginning to feel something that had been absent from his own life for a long time: hope.

I looked over to Michelle and said, "We're going to do this."

Magic and I left that night like we had just won a Championship. We were going to help Dennis return to the NBA.

The thing about Magic Johnson is that he follows up on his ideas. Like my father used to say, "The idea is only one percent." Magic knew how to give the other 99 percent.

He invited Dennis to the 24-Hour Fitness opening the next day. Dennis walked out on stage from behind the curtain, and the crowd went wild. I knew right then that if Dennis followed through on all of his plans, he would be as big of a player as he ever was.

The fans went crazy for Dennis. You could just see and feel the energy of how people felt about him. Dennis and Magic were complete opposites: Magic is the most extroverted person you would ever meet, and Dennis the most introverted. As soon as Dennis waved, he turned around and walked right back to the backstage area.

I could tell Magic was a little stunned, but ever the showman he kept going.

I immediately went backstage to talk to Dennis. I could tell he was sober. I didn't realize until later that being sober was the problem. I couldn't get up in front of people sober either, and I had nowhere near the fame and celebrity of Dennis Rodman. I did not experience the same kind of hunger from fans or the pressure of the spotlight.

Celebrity helps some people come alive.

For others, it's downright terrifying.

Despite Dennis' actions, I thought that once we got him back on the court, the one place where he was comfortable, everything would be different.

Magic arranged for Dennis to join his guys practicing at UCLA. Dennis called me the night before. I could tell he was drunk as he explained that he couldn't go.

"Alright," I said. "I'll call Magic and tell him you can't make it. Just make sure you get to the next one."

Epic Ali-Frazier reunion dinner in Philadelphia, here in Muhammad's hotel suite the night before the NBA All-Star game in 2002.

Still so surreal looking at this photo with the two Kings, Ali and Frazier, sitting courtside for the 2002 NBA All-Star game in Philadelphia. Headlines around the world said "Ali-Frazier - A Peace of History". What a blessing and a privilege to be right next to them and be a part of it. These two were the stars of stars that night, just as they were in any room they ever walked into. You can see in my eyes I wasn't exactly sober. I just didn't feel worthy back then of sitting there with the two Global Kings.

Myself, Magic and Mom at the Turning Point Rehab Gala in 2013. Magic flew in to be honored and helped raise a lot of money that evening.

In good company with Dennis Rodman and Mickey Rourke at a Foot Locker charity event in NYC in 2009.

The first time I worked with Dennis at a signing in Anaheim, California in 1996.

One of the rare times these legendary PMG clients, Hulk Hogan and Ric Flair, appeared together.

Proud to be with my spiritual brother, Chris Herren, when he was the honoree for the Turning Point Gala in 2015.

Performing together with PMG Client and Motley Crue Frontman Vince Neil at Turning Point Gala in 2015. (Photo credit: Fred Fogg)

What a thrill this was for me as a lifelong and diehard San Diego Chargers fan. Smokin' Joe Frazier was honored on the field after kick-off on October 1, 2010. It was the 35th anniversary of Ali-Frazier III "Thrilla in Manila". Also pictured is my good friend, Frosty, of almost 30 years.

My sister Stacey and I surprised Mom and Dad for their 50th wedding anniversary in NYC in 2015. What a blessing to be there sober and present for it.

Hulkster appeared on the field courtesy of longtime corporate client 800-Loan-Mart at the Chargers-Patriots Sunday night game in 2015.

Here I am in 1999 with Pamela Anderson at her first convention appearance in Atlanta, Georgia. She said she had a great experience with me and my team at PMG handling everything.

Me appearing on Dr OZ with Darryl Strawberry in November of 2017 talking about addiction recovery. Such a gift to have different platforms like this to be able to show others hope! And to educate the youth to not ever start based on my experiences and where it took me.

One of my many Christmas/New Year trips to the Bahamas to get to spend time with Earvin and his family.

Iconic photo in 2009 at an Affliction appearance in Tampa with Smokin Joe Frazier, Micky Ward, Chuck Zito and Vinny Paz.

An epic photo of me and Frosty at the 1992 Pasadena Super Bowl featuring the Cowboys vs Bills with Michael Jackson performing at halftime (Great photo skills by my boy Mark Adrian).

At the Mayweather-Corrales Fight in Vegas. You can tell by looking at my eyes I wasn't exactly sober here.

Getting ready for a global press conference in September, 2013 with sponsor Paddy Power after Dennis returned from North Korea.

Me and the best big 3 ever at Michael Jordan's Basketball Hall of Fame induction after party in 2009. (Jordan, Pippen, and Rodman)

NJ Mental Health Association Gala in May of 2015 I was privileged to be the honoree. Being interviewed here on red carpet by award winning reporter Steve Adubato.

First time meeting and working with longtime client Chevy Chase in White Plains, NY.

Nothing like our Father's Day fishing trips. Dad is wearing the hat from the life changing 1996 fishing trip we went on in Alaska. He always wanted me to write a book trying to help and inspire others so I know he is looking down smiling.

What a great dinner this was with these Legends and clients at the Bel-Air hotel earlier this year. Dennis and Charlie never had dinner together so Nicky C and I set it up.

Here I am with Dennis on the set of a campaign he filmed for WeBet88.com, an online casino he endorsed in China.

At a signing in Indianapolis that we booked for Larry Bird in December of 2016.

Dennis came to visit Hulk and I in January of 2016 during a commercial shoot with 800 Loan Mart in Los Angeles.

On the set of Celebrity Apprentice All Stars with the now President Trump.

At a charity event with the legendary Gary Vaynerchuk at my boy Eytan Sugarman's amazing restaurant, Hunt and Fish Club, in NYC.

My first time working with Pam in 1996 at the Four Seasons Hotel in Beverly Hills I booked her first signing. Tommy showed up and she was pregnant with her first baby. They were awesome – two great people.

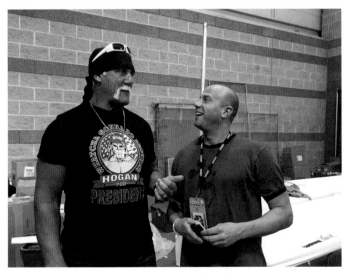

In Atlantic City at a convention with Hulk in 2016 discussing the thought of him running for President. (Great photo skills by Ron Howard)

Priscilla and I were one of 100 guests invited to Magic's surprise 25th wedding anniversary for Cookie. The festivities started in Monaco and went on for 10 days around Europe. What an epic trip! Thanks Magic & Cookie!

My second family – David, Becky and Mom Marion Deutsch. So much love for them.

My second Father – Uncle Stewart. I can't put into words what this man means to me.

Love working with this legend. Burt Reynolds has always been first class over the years.

Grandma Francis and Poppy Herman probably back in 1973 with me and Stacey.

Such a great photo with these two bad boys at a convention in New York in 2017. PMG has had the privilege of working with Mike Tyson on several occasions over the years. The Champ has always been amazing.

Great meeting with 2 of our biggest and newest clients. Acting legend Charlie Sheen and Shark Tank mogul Kevin Harrington. This was a power business meeting at Charlie's home in 2017.

With client Pound for Pound King 9 x Champ Roy Jones Jr and our girl Mercedes Ganon. Getting ready for a press tour in NYC to promote the Star Vizn instructional video project PMG put together to learn how to box and train like The Champ!

My man and publishing mogul Jason Binn. Has supported me since day one and we go back 25 plus years.

The God Moment at the US landmark Dr Bob's house on my 9 year sober b-day having this man greet me on the steps wearing that shirt after all I talked about on the way over was how proud my Dad is and he just passed away 5 months earlier.

Always a pleasure working with these two clients, Michael O'keefe and Cindy Morgan, and stars of the iconic film, Caddyshack.

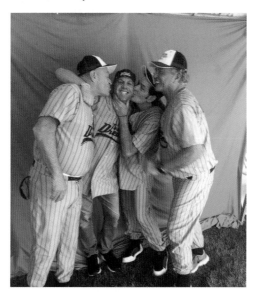

Historic reunion we pulled off at PMG here with cast of the Major League movie clients Charlie Sheen, Corbin Bernsen an Tom Berenger. This was at MAB's Team of Dreams Celebrity softball game played at the real Field of Dreams in Dubuque.

Priscilla, Magic, Cookie and I in September of 2017 in Los Angeles celebrating with 100 of their closest friends the 25th anniversary trip to Monaco from September 2016. So many friendships were made during that trip which will last a lifetime.

Spending time with longtime client and friend, Chevy Chase, in London on behalf of corporate clients Rocco and Ant in January of 2018 for a sold out theatre show with 3000 fans.

In Chicago with PMG clients that happen to be two of the best NBA dunkers ever, Dominique Wilkins and Spud Webb. It was great to book them together in November of 2017 for the first time.

My Dream Team publisher and writer Anna David and Kristen McGuiness Much love to both of them for bringing this project to life xoxo.

Another spiritual brother for public addiction advocacy –
The Dope Man, Tim Ryan.

What a privilege this was hanging out with client Evel Knievel
in Butte, Montana in 2005 before we signed a slot machine
licensing deal and a commercial for eBay. I was blessed to
work with him and become good friends for a few years
before he passed. PMG/Steve has since negotiated numerous
licensing projects under the Evel Knievel name to keep his
legacy alive.

At my official PMG launch party in Atlanta, GA with clients Pamela Anderson, Chuck Zito and the Joe Frazier back in 1999.

WOW! At my 40th b-day at Tao in NYC. What a privilege that Magic, Dennis and Smokin Joe all came in for it. The real blessing is that I was sober and in my second year of sobriety. To be in the moment and be present and take in such an evening was amazing.

Another spiritual brother who's changing the game of public advocacy for addiction recovery - Ryan Hampton. Here we are at the White House in March of 2018 for the President's Opioid Summit. We were both privileged to be invited to and be a part of it.

Priscilla and I on our second trip to the White in 2018 for the Opioid Summit.

My brothers and PMG agents Nicky C and VO. So much love for both of them.

My freshman year at University of Bridgeport. Not a good sign after starting steroids for the first time. My boy Jared Lerner being carried while my best friend Jonathan Erde looks on.

Team PMG holiday lunch with Nicky C, VO, Steve and Jonathan back in 2015.

Sponsor Stephen Della Valle changed and saved my life, but I prefer to call him my big spiritual brother.

Three of my boys. I go back almost 40 years with Rob Belcuore and Greg Bruno, and Alan Elwood was there in the beginning of the Prince Marketing Group launch in 1996. Much love to you guys.

What a memory! My good friend Dean and I bought our way into Super Bowl XXV through a couple of vendors. We were on the field the entire first half and right by Whitney Houston after she sang the best rendition ever of the Star Spangled Banner. Sadly, we were arrested at halftime due to heightened security with the ongoing Persian Gulf War. Thankfully, we were released without charges and just made it back in time to our hotel to watch Scott Nor-Wides kick sail right and the Giants won the Super Bowl. The FBI agent let me keep this as we were escorted out of the stadium so I could always share the story with others.

Me holding one of the three T-206 super rare Honus Wagner baseball cards I bought and sold. This was back in 1990. I sold it back then for $70,000. If only I saved it! It's probably worth close to $1.0M now or more!!

Me with two of my closest friends. I go back 35 years with Frank Basile. And Mike "Berto" Bertolini and I met in 1996 when he gave me a chance after others turned their back on me after I made a major mistake. Love both of these guys as they've never judged me and have always been there.

Great guy Joe Manganiello. Always cool to work with but even a better person.

Me and my beautiful fur baby Rodney Frazier Prince (Courtesy of Tuck-N-Roll Acres).

Two amazing influential men in my life. My late father, Martin Prince, and Harlan Werner aka HJW.

Love these 3, we have been friends for over 40 years. You know it's real friendship when we can make fun of each other all the time and keep laughing. They have been with me through all the highs and lows and in betweens. David Elwood, Mark Schachter and Andrew Wayne - much love to you guys and your families.

Great event we booked in January of 2013 for the GOAT, Joe Montana, at Hard Rock Seminole in Hollywood Florida. I also met my man Mike AKA Canada Bob that night who is part of our tight inner circle now at PMG. Love you sweetheart!

With good friend and client for 17 plus years Brande Roderick, who has a huge heart. She's also had an incredible career from Baywatch, Playboy Playmate of the Year, Celebrity Apprentice on two different seasons, Starsky & Hutch, and as an accomplished writer.

Hanging with Hulkster in his trailer on the set of the Radio Shack Super Bowl commercial we booked for him in January 2014. Look at those pythons!

What a mess this interview was on Anderson Cooper when Evel Knievel passed away. I was trying to detox from opiates 24 hours before it and was so sick.

In Atlantic City at the Iconic 500 Homerun Club Member convention in 1989, where Reggie Jackson bought his rookie card from me.

Here I am with Dennis in Washington, DC for the March for Our Lives historic rally with powerhouse music manager and Industry Icon/Entrepreneur Scooter Braun.

Dennis, VO and I with Jimmy Fallon at the March for Our
Lives walk in DC. Jimmy has always done right by Dennis
in his late night talk show. Great Guy!

3 of the most special men in my life – Dad, Uncle Stew and
Nicky C at dinner a few years ago

Another spiritual brother who has changed the public recovery advocacy game Greg Williams, Anonymous People documentary director and Facing Addiction.

The Boss making is easy for me and business partner Ryan Schinman flying back to Cali on Air Magic after a big keynote speech for Oracle Netsuite in Vegas, April 2018.

Me being honored and giving my speech at the Turning Point Drug and Alcohol rehab Gala in October of 2017. What a privilege for me!

With Dr Drew and Andrew Giuliani from the Trump administration at the historic Opioid Crisis Summit at the White House in February.

Great corporate event we booked for a social media firm in January in NYC for the GOAT Jerry Rice. He's as classy and professional off the field as he was on it.

Once in a lifetime weekend in April 2011 when the Detroit Pistons finally retired Dennis's Jersey #. You can see how big the smile is on my face sitting behind Dennis and next to Steve. No one knew it but three days later he would also be introduced on the court at halftime of the NCAA Final Four National Championship game as a Naismith Basketball Hall of Fame inductee.

Cannabis firm's exposure from Dennis Rodman trip hailed as 'truly genius' marketing

Former NBA basketball player Dennis Rodman arrives at Beijing Capital International Airport in Beijing on June 13. (Mark Schiefelbein, Associated Press)

By John Schrover

Dennis's last trip to North Korea was in June of 2017. Our friends at Pot Coin.com got behind his mission and sponsored the trip. It seemed to be a hit in the Global media.

Smokin' Stylish Seriously Punch.

SURGEON GENERAL WARNING: Cigars Are Not A Safe Alternative To Cigarettes.

We pitched Smokin Joe to Punch Cigars and landed this national print ad campaign in 2000.

S2 and I at the Saints-Chargers game on the field at the Superdome back in 2012. He's a 40 year die-hard Saint fan and me being the same longtime Charger fan we had to go. Sadly my team choked as always and he walked out victorious.

My beautiful Mom and I at her 75th birthday in February 2018. My sister Stacey who has had a great career as an event planner organized an epic birthday dinner for our family and close friends. I know that my dad was there with us in spirit.

Here on the set of Star Vizn fitness video shoot with Housewives franchise Royalty Joe and Melissa Gorga (NJ Housewives). Two beautiful people inside and out that have been a pleasure to work with and call friends.

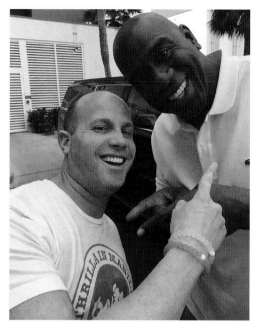

A great selfie with the Magic Man in Las Vegas before the Mayweather-Pacquio fight.

Was amazing to see Michael Jackson's Super Bowl XXVII performance at the Rose Bowl. In the early 2000's Michael, Magic, Smokin Joe and I almost became partners in a new agency called the Prince World Marketing Group. It was incredibly surreal talking to Michael, I still have his voice mail messages. We were unable to make a deal but was still an amazing experience.

"I'm a huge Dead Head been to over 100 shows. Now I go as a wharf rat which is a person in recovery who is still a fan of the music. I was given this 7 year chip at the legendary show I went to with my boy Van on July 4, 2015. What a gift this was from the leader of the Wharf Rat meeting at the Chicago show for the bands Fare Thee Well finale tour after 50 years. I've also gone completely deaf with nerve damage in my left ear since I was 25 years old doctors never really figured out if it was all that loud music or excessive opiate abuse."

I got him another practice date. This time, he didn't even call me to say he wasn't going. I found out from Magic.

It still wasn't the final strike.

That summer, Jimmy Kimmel launched his late-night talk show from El Capitan Theater in the heart of Hollywood. He chose Magic Johnson as his first guest, the man who had come to embody LA over the past 20 years.

Magic invited Dennis to join him. Magic knew the power of media, and he knew how important the show might have been in helping Dennis to make an NBA comeback.

I arranged everything—the car, the driver—and I worked with Michelle to keep Dennis on target.

I knew we had one last real shot at this, and if Dennis could land it, we might be on our way back to the NBA. Dennis called me that afternoon. I knew he was drunk, even though he told me he was sick. He just couldn't make it.

It was two hours before the show when I called Magic to tell him. It might have been one of the hardest calls of my career. I was the one who had asked Magic to give Dennis a chance, and in his typical way he had gone above and beyond to make that happen. I had used my own personal and professional chips to give Dennis this shot. Despite all of his promises, he wasn't able to show up. I felt like it was as much my fault as it was his.

Magic told me, "I don't know, Darren. You have your hands full there with Dennis. Just make sure you protect yourself. He is definitely a full-time job, and you can't handle him alone."

Here's the thing. I understood Dennis. Though I couldn't understand my own addiction at the time, I could understand his drinking. I felt for him. I knew that underneath the booze and the partying and sunglasses, he didn't want this to be his life. Dennis genuinely wanted to get back to the game, but the booze was in control. Alcohol was making all of Dennis' bad decisions for him.

The worst part was that at the end of summer, I was going to have Dennis and Magic at the same event. I wasn't looking forward to it. We had already contracted Dennis for a charity event in the Hamptons that August, so both men would be together soon enough.

It was a mess. On one hand, I had Magic there being Magic. He put in twice the work and was a gentleman to everyone. On the other hand, Dennis was more into the open bar than he was the crowd. I kept trying to cover for him, but the game was up. At least, I thought it was.

Magic Johnson was one persistent man, and he did really care about Dennis. After the tournament, Magic told me that his business partner at the time, Seattle Supersonics and Starbucks founder Howard Schultz, wanted to have a meeting with us at his Hamptons estate. I almost said no, fearful of what would happen. Did I really need another embarrassment, especially in front of a billionaire?

It was my job to let Dennis know, and he seemed genuinely excited about the meeting. He showed up sober and was the same Dennis that Magic and I had met at the restaurant: honest, driven, and raw about his fears but also his strengths. I could tell that Schultz was impressed. He had heard all of the stories about the man, but in that moment Dennis was simply someone who thrived at playing basketball. He was clearly in it for the love of the game.

Many have since argued that Schultz was not. I'm not sure that's why it didn't work out. Despite liking Dennis and telling Magic how impressed he was, Schultz decided it wasn't a fit. Dennis was disappointed, but that meeting cemented my desire to work with him.

I told him we would find another opportunity. We just needed to find someone who could manage Dennis. That's where Thaer Mustafa came in. We met him at the Hamptons charity event. He was one of Dennis' good friends, a bit rough around the edges but he knew how to keep people in line. As Thaer said, "If you want Dennis to work at maximum efficiency, you need a guy like me."

Thaer came on as Dennis' full-time handler. It was his job to get Dennis where he needed to be, on time, and when possible, sober. I began to look for other opportunities outside of the NBA, knowing that the goal was always to get Dennis back there.

Magic was a testament to what could happen after NBA retirement. He turned his brand into an empire. While clearly Dennis and Magic had very different brands, there was no reason Dennis couldn't do the same. If only he could stay out of his own way.

Thaer and I began working together to build Dennis a new team. As Thaer said at the time, "I don't like agents, but you're not an agent."

I understood what he meant. I didn't do the work for my cut. I did it because I believed in my clients. I knew Dennis could still create a post-retirement career. I believed that he could return to the game he loved so much.

We started getting Dennis out for PR opportunities. He would make appearances at celebrity basketball events. He started doing the trade show circuit and corporate appearances, red carpet events, and launch parties. When he was sober he was a more subdued, gentler Dennis. Other times, he was the life of the party.

Sometimes, he was a downright mess.

In 2002, I booked Dennis on the *The Best Damn Sports Show* with Tom Arnold and Dennis' former teammate, John Salley. He did the pre-interview from his house and was completely fine. I was looking forward to the interview, thinking it might help to pump up the argument for his return. An hour before the show was supposed to tape, Dennis excused himself to go buy some tacos for the production staff. Thirty minutes later, he hadn't returned, and we knew something was up. When he finally walked into the house, he was a hot mess. In addition to picking up tacos, he had done a bunch of tequila shots at the Mexican restaurant. There was nothing I could do but watch him bomb.

I thought back to all of the times I had seen this happen: the Kimmel taping, the Hamptons, and now this. I had to accept it. As much as I loved Dennis Rodman like a brother, I couldn't trust him. Magic was right. I needed to protect myself.

At this point, I was so deep into Dennis' drama that my own addiction issues had taken a backseat. My using had continued unnoticed. It was so much easier to focus on Dennis' issues. Even as I polished off a bottle of vodka right alongside him at the club, I thought I was fine. I would get up the next day and get the job done.

No problem.

Then, we got a much-needed break for Dennis' career.

A few months later, we got a call from *Celebrity Mole*. They were interested in having Dennis on the show. I sent Thaer and Dennis to the first meeting in Newport Beach. When they returned, they both seemed happy about the interview, but I got a call the next day from the casting agent, Robin Roth. She told me it did not go well.

"What happened?" I asked, confused.

"Dennis told them that the show sucked. He couldn't seem less interested."

I called Dennis and Thaer immediately. He told me that the producers were a bunch of bums. They showed up wearing ripped shorts and driving some shitty rental car. Dennis had been swindled enough times in his life. He couldn't take these guys seriously.

I called Robin back with Thaer and asked for another meeting. Oddly enough, after Robin pleaded her case to the producers, they cast Dennis for the show, which he ultimately won.

That's the thing about Dennis. When he wants to put on a good show, he puts on the best show. If he's not interested, there's nothing you can do to engage him. Dennis was on the show with Corbin Bernsen, who was famous for his days on *LA Law* and his role in the movie *Major League* with Charlie Sheen. He has become a good friend and client over the years.

Ahmad Rashad was hosting the show and began to talk to Dennis about that long-anticipated NBA comeback. After that, Dennis suddenly started taking his comeback seriously again. He quit drinking and started going to the gym twice a day. This was the first time since we began working together when he seemed truly ready for an NBA comeback. However, if I was going to try to negotiate a deal for him, I still needed to get that certification from the NBA.

I wound up setting up a call with David Stern and Russ Granik, the Commissioner and Deputy Commissioner of the NBA. I was stressed for the call. Not only had I never negotiated an NBA contract; I was also trying to sell a player who wasn't entirely welcome in the NBA.

"Look, Dennis is sober and he's committed," I explained to them. "He's been in the gym twice a day, getting in shape. He wants to do this the right way."

"Don't worry," I added, referring to Dennis' promise in his book, *Bad as I Want to Be.* "He's not going to walk off the court naked, put a dress on you, David, and sing 'I Did It My Way.'"

We all laughed.

After that call, Dennis was less optimistic. He told me, "They're going to tell me what they're going to tell me, but I know they don't want me back in the league."

Dennis had so many people supporting him—Isaiah Thomas, Scottie Pippen, and John Salley. Many people were working to get him back in the league, and we finally had a team that was interested: the Denver Nuggets.

Five years before, I had been selling collectibles at memorabilia conventions. Now, I was meeting with Howard Schultz and Kiki VanDeWeghe, the General Manager of the Nuggets and a former baller himself, working to get Dennis Rodman back in the NBA. The Nuggets didn't sign him, but Dennis' career seemed to be heating up.

That same year, we got a call from Lorne Michaels' production company, Broadway Video, and Mess Media about doing a show at ESPN on Dennis' return to the NBA. I reconnected with Ryan Schinman, who was then at the height of Platinum Rye. He gave us a great review on Dennis' brand and where it should be with a successful NBA comeback. I felt certain that with all of these powerful people behind us, we were about to take off to the next level.

The only problem was that Dennis began drinking again.

He was only a few weeks into filming the show when I got a call from the producer.

"Darren," the frustrated producer explained. "We're getting crap here. When is Dennis going to give us some good, sober footage?"

I wasn't sure if I could promise anything. I had learned by now that I couldn't make guarantees for Dennis when he was drinking.

Then I got the call from Phil Jackson. It was late on a Saturday evening when he called me at home. He had recently moved to the Lakers. Kobe was there, Shaq was gone, and with it, the drama that had been so problematic for Dennis years before. He said he would consider sending out his assistant coach, Tex Winter, to come watch Dennis working out.

Tex Winter was a legend, on and off the court. He was the one responsible for the famed Triangle Offense. Tex was in his sixties when he joined the Bulls and was well into his eighties when he continued his record-setting career with Jackson on the Lakers. The man was a legend.

Tex had also worked with Dennis on the Bulls. These were guys who knew and loved Dennis. If anyone could manage him, it was Phil and Tex.

Six hours later, I got a call from Thaer. It was four in the morning. He said, "Your client just fucked himself up for good this time."

There had been an accident in Vegas. Dennis has flipped his motorcycle outside of the strip club Treasures. He was in the hospital with sixty stitches in his shin, but the real ending to his NBA dream came in the form of a DUI.

For those of us who loved Dennis, our hearts were broken. At this point, he had a wife and two small children. We all knew how important that meeting could have been with the Lakers, and I had just told Phil that Dennis had slowed down on the drinking and was doing a lot better.

A part of me couldn't help but wish that I had been there, but I also knew from experience that none of us could protect Dennis from himself.

Thaer, myself, and Dennis' other long-term bodyguard, Wendell "Big Will" Williams, knew it was time to do something. Dennis was becoming a pariah. He would arrive at events, and people would try to get away from him. I once watched P. Diddy literally run in the other direction. This wasn't the Dennis we knew. We told him, "You're either going to get shot or you're going to end up dead or in jail. Either way, you're on your way to losing everything. It's either time to get your shit together or we're all out."

At that point, we were as close with Dennis as his family. Dennis nodded quietly. The next day, he quit drinking. For the next 18 months, he was on the wagon. Though I still couldn't accept it, I should have done the same thing myself.

Chapter Eight

SHOULDERS OF GIANTS

WHILE DENNIS STAYED SOBER, MY USING INCREASED.

I would find myself nodding off in meetings and falling asleep in the back seat of a limo next to a client. I was always on the road, flying from LA to New York to London. I would get home from China only to leave the next morning for Florida. Who could blame me if I took a little catnap on the way to the airport?

I chalked it up to the price of running a busy marketing agency, which only seemed to be getting bigger.

I didn't think the pills were a problem. I thought it was just a staffing issue. Even though my business was growing, the size of my team remained the same. I still only had two assistants in the office. I didn't realize that I could have had other Darren Princes doing the work alongside me, that I didn't need to be the only one. So, instead I just became completely overwhelmed, dealing with Dennis and his mayhem and trying to handle all of my other clients. I had started working with the other *Baywatch* beauties as well, including Carmen Electra and Brande Roderick. I also started arranging events for Motley Crue's Vince Neil, booking him for promotional and private appearances as well as for business opportunities.

I was exhausted, and it wasn't just from the pills and the partying.

Then, I added one of the biggest names in the world to my client list: Terry Gene Bollea, otherwise known as Hulk Hogan.

While I had contacted Hulk before, he hadn't been interested. But his attorney, Henry Holmes also represented Pamela Anderson and because of that connection, I was able to negotiate a small licensing deal for Hulk with a trading card opportunity. The next year, I booked him for a corporate eyewear appearance with my friend, Gary Martin, at Revolution Eyewear. These weren't multi-million-dollar deals, but it showed Hulk that I knew what I was doing. He could see that I had connections, and that he could trust me.

After these two opportunities, I approached Henry to see if he could reconnect me with Hulk. He told me to try Hulk directly. Two days later, Hulk and I spoke over the phone to talk about Prince Marketing Group and his career.

Hulk was regarded by many as the greatest professional wrestler of all time. He wasn't just a wrestler. He was a brand name; he was recognized across the world. He was the King of Kings and had the world's cleanest image. At the time, he had been married for over 20 years and had raised two beautiful children. This was the early 2000s, and the Hogan family's reality show, *Hogan Knows Best*, was a smash hit on TV. Hogan was as famous for his 30-year career in wrestling as he was for his larger-than-life personality. And like Magic, he could be counted on. He knew how to perform, and he could work a crowd like the best of them. He is the best of them.

On that first call, Hulk asked how Dennis was doing. Back in the late 1990s, they had been tag-team partners on the new World order (nWo) team during the World Championship Wrestling (WCW) heyday. I told Hulk that Dennis was sober, working again to get back into the NBA.

By the end of the conversation, I had added Hulk Hogan as a PMG client.

Two months later, I got another great call. The American Basketball Association was interested in Dennis. He had been sober for a year and was ready for another change. They wanted him to play for the Long Beach Jam. He joined and brought to the team what we had promised so many others: talent, energy, and crowds.

That year, the Long Beach Jam won the championship.

After years of feeling like I was swimming in mayhem, life actually began to settle down.

That year, I hired my childhood friend Steve Simon (who had shared the table with me at that first baseball show). The first thing he did was to book a Super Bowl appearance for Magic. He nailed every element of the job. For the first time, I realized that I didn't have to be the only Darren Prince at PMG.

Steve Simon started reaching out for new leads and new corporations. At the same time, I had started working more with

Nicky C. I was building a team, and it felt good. We immediately started bringing in deals for Hulk Hogan. Opportunities were hot for Magic, Smokin' Joe, and Dennis. Dennis was doing great on the Long Beach Jam.

I could actually begin to breathe.

I even met a girl.

I had gone on plenty of dates at that point and dated plenty of beautiful women, but I knew from the minute I saw Symone that she was different. I had met her the year before at an eyewear convention I had attended with Dennis. A few months later, we met for lunch in LA. She was pretty and kind and a lot of fun to be around, but I also realized on that very first date that she was a much straighter arrow than I was. We were drinking champagne at lunch when I pulled out my Vicodin prescription. That's right. It was a beautiful, sunny day in LA. I had the perfect date, and I was the idiot who asked her if she wanted to pop a Vicodin.

Symone should have known right then there was a problem, but she just looked at me like I had three eyes and asked, "Why would you take painkillers?"

It was a question I had begun asking myself.

While there was no way I was ready to accept that I had a problem, I had begun to see that the pills were becoming one. The bigger my client list became and larger the events I was organizing, the more opportunities I was getting to succeed... and fail. I was starting to realize that popping a pill every few hours was not a recipe for success.

It was 2002, the year of that famous Ali-Frazier reunion and that amazing night in Philadelphia when I got to bring two of the greatest men in sports and in history together. I was high for the entire experience.

I remembered that night at the hotel in Philadelphia, going up to Ali's room on the elevator with Smokin' Joe, wondering what it might be like to actually ditch the pills. What might happen if I tried to be present for the history I was watching first hand?

I really don't think I had ever thought much about being present. When you are in your twenties, sitting at the VIP table in a strip club, popping bottles and pills, you think you are embracing the present. I always had the sense that you only live once, so I thought I was participating in my life by taking advantage of every opportunity: the good, the bad, and the ugly.

As I was getting older, I was beginning to realize that I needed to change the way I was living. I was working with important people on important deals. I had a bigger responsibility to them than I had been willing to accept. Standing in that hotel room with Joe and Muhammad Ali, the weight of my choices felt as serious as life and death.

Harlan Werner, Ali's marketing agent and one of my mentors, had been the one to coordinate the meeting with me, but he ended up getting stuck at an event in Las Vegas.

"You got this," Harlan told me before I headed over to pick up Joe. I wasn't sure that I did.

That night in Ali's hotel room, after the two Champs hugged, we all sat down for dinner. It was like eating at the king's table.

Lonnie acted like Joe was an old friend, offering him different food suggestions for his diabetes.

Once the food came, everyone started eating. In the middle of dinner, Ali looked up and started shaking his fist at Joe. He smiled and bit his bottom lip as he joked. He reminded me of Billy Crystal's famous set about Ali. "Joe, Fraaazier, Joe Fraaazier, I want you Joe Fraaazier!"

Joe laughed, "Man, didn't I kick your black ass enough? We just made up 15 minutes ago. We can't keep on fighting."

Everyone was hysterical.

Despite the joke, the rivalry was still there. There was just this fight in both of them. Even at the dinner table with no cameras, they couldn't seem to hold back.

Before we left, we all got together and took pictures. Joe's son, Marvis, began to lead us in a prayer, but then Joe interrupted him. As Joe held Ali's hand, he prayed, "Dear Lord, we have forgotten, and we have forgiven. We ask that you heal this man who has done so much for this world so he can be there for his family and children and all his fans that love him around the world."

In all the years I had worked with Smokin' Joe, I had never seen him cry, but that night tears fell from his eyes. We all cried, as 30 years of bitterness and anger finally disappeared between Muhammad Ali and Smokin' Joe Frazier.

I left the night wondering how I had just gotten the privilege to be a witness to history. Me? Darren Prince, a special ed kid from

New Jersey. On top of it all, I couldn't stop getting high. They say one spiritual experience can change everything. Well, that night was like watching the hand of God reach out and reunite two of the biggest giants in the world.

I promised myself that I would throw the pills away the next day. I couldn't keep this secret anymore. There was simply too much on the line.

But then tomorrow came, and tomorrow was always the same.

The morning after our visit to Ali's room, I got a call from the NBA, who must have heard that something had gone down with Joe and Muhammad the night before. I denied that anything had happened, but when they asked if Joe would be okay sitting near Muhammad at the NBA All-Star Game I said that would be fine. I didn't tell Joe, just in case it didn't happen, because I wanted him to be surprised if it did.

Almost 80 percent of my job was to manage people's expectations. I had to say just enough to get someone to show up, but I didn't want to sell an idea too hard in case it didn't come through. I was negotiating a fine balance between promise and negotiation. It was an exhausting exercise. After getting off the phone with the NBA, I could feel my sciatica flaring up.

It always worked that way. I would think I could live without the pills. Then, something stressful would happen, and it was like the pain would go from two to 10 within seconds. Whatever promise I had made that amazing night went straight out the window. How was I going to get through such a big night without my painkillers?

Though I didn't answer Symone's question that day when she asked me why I would take painkillers, the answer was simple: to make me feel like I was enough.

The night of the NBA All-Star Game, I arrived at the arena with Smokin' Joe and Nicky C. We were escorted to courtside seats, center court. As soon as the crowd saw Joe, they went wild, screaming, "Smokin' Joe! Smokin' Joe! Frazier! Frazier!"

I still remember years later, Harlan telling me that he felt bad that Ali had received all the accolades. As I told Harlan, he just never saw it from Joe's side.

"You were always with Ali," I told him. "But everywhere I went with Joe he was a superstar. Everyone wanted to meet him and shake his hand. People just didn't know about it as much as they did with Ali."

That night was proof that 30 years after his most famous bouts, Smokin' Joe Frazier could still rile an arena.

As we made our way courtside, I didn't say anything, though in the back of my mind I knew why we had the best seats in the house.

We sat down and suddenly began to hear the chants, "Ali! Ali! Ali!"

Joe looked around and said to me, "Is the Butterfly here?"

From behind, Ali was walking down the aisle. He was wearing this red polo and he was with his best friend and photographer, Howard Bingham. Howard was sitting in Seat One; Ali was in Seat Two; I was in Seat Three; Joe in Four; and Nicky C. in Five.

Ali gave me a big hug and grabbed Joe's hand before sitting down.

Joe leaned over and said, "Switch with me, boss man. Give me your seat."

Alicia Keys had just taken the stage to sing "America the Beautiful," and I was like, "Oh shit! This is happening." I quickly swapped with Joe.

By this time, all of the cameras were on Ali and Joe sitting next to each other, holding one another's arms.

Tears ran down my face. I knew that over 140 countries in the world were now witnessing the history I had seen the night before.

The roar was deafening, and the whole stadium jumped to their feet to give the men a standing ovation.

Everyone was going crazy. Magic and his wife, Cookie, were sitting five seats to my left. Justin Timberlake, Britney Spears, Kobe Bryant, Michael Jordan, P-Diddy, and Allen Iverson were all standing there with huge smiles on their faces. Everyone was in awe of what was happening.

I remember thinking, "These are the king of kings. In their presence, even the biggest stars became kids."

So, you can only imagine what that made someone like me feel like. I slipped two pills in my mouth, careful that the cameras didn't catch me, and began to chew them, once again looking for my escape.

Finally, after the roar died down, the two men leaned into each other.

I heard Ali say, "Hey, Champ."

Joe replied, "Yeah, Champ."

These two men had spent decades denying one another's greatness. In that moment, as calm and cool as could be, they finally acknowledged one another as equals.

"We're still two bad brothers, aren't we?" Ali asked.

Joe laughed softly, putting his hand on Ali's. "Yes we are, man. Yes we are."

In that moment, I realized that they were men of their time, and the world would never make two of them again.

Six months later, they walked the red carpet together for the ESPYs, and Harlan Werner was able to be there.

The last time they were together was in 2005. They did a photo shoot together for *Sports Illustrated* at Joe's gym in Philadelphia. They were both getting older and weaker. They held on a little tighter when they hugged that day. Probably no one on earth understood those two men the way they understood each other; where they came from, what they went through, and what they both achieved.

To this day, there is probably no greater success in my life than being a part of that reunion. It would have been the crowning achievement for any agent. The two kings of boxing; the greatest rivalry of any sport; the stars of any room they ever walked into.

Ali and Frazier were brought back together, and I was there to witness the event.

I was 32 years old. After a few rough years, I felt like I was back on top of my game. Being in the middle of all those photos with legends Ali and Frazier brought me even more business. I worked really hard to be humble. The only reason I was there was that I was trusted by Joe, and Harlan, and the Ali family.

For years, I never told anyone the story of that night. Word got out, though, and people knew I was there. Being a part of history definitely helped PMG to gain more credibility.

The pills, on the other hand, had other plans.

After the reunion, the pills just weren't working like they used to. No matter how much I drank or how many pills I took, I just couldn't achieve the same effect. I could no longer take over a room. For years when I was using the drugs, I felt like I was on top of the world. Now the drugs were on top of me, and I was suffocating.

I don't know if it was because I had tried to quit that weekend in Philadelphia with Ali and Joe, or that witnessing their reunion had been my first spiritual experience.

I had built my business on the shaky ground of low self-esteem, and no matter how much energy I poured into it, I could feel the foundation crumbling. Anxiety was fast taking the place of any sense of confidence. I kept trying different ways of taking opiates—snorting them, dissolving them under my tongue— anything to get back my old high, but nothing worked. I was miserable, and I didn't know what to do.

I couldn't accept the fact that I needed to quit. I didn't comprehend what that meant, and I was still years away from understanding how to do it.

Towards the end of the year, I went to the World Series with my best friend, Jonathan Erde. Jonathan was an obsessive Boston Red Sox fan, and that was the year the Sox finally broke their World Series curse. We had amazing seats, and I knew how much the series meant to John. Not long into the game, I couldn't sit still. I got up and started to leave.

John said, "Where the heck are you going?"

"I'm going to get something to eat," I told him, and I did. I walked straight out of the stadium and to a restaurant around the corner, where I watched the rest of the game by myself.

I didn't know what to do. For 20 years, pills had been my best friend. They had been giving me my super powers to perform, and suddenly they had become my Kryptonite.

Later that night, after John and I reunited, I lied and told him I had run into some friends and watched the rest of the game with them. I ignored the fact that I was basically telling him that I ditched him at the World Series, but it was better than the truth.

What I had begun to realize was that if I used right before bed and then woke up six, or even worse, eight hours later, I would experience the first throws of withdrawal. I would vomit first thing in the morning or wake up with terrible shakes. My solution was to set an alarm at 3am, take the pills, do some work, and then try to crash out until morning. With this routine, when I woke up later that morning the pills would still be in my system.

That night in Boston, John and I were staying in the same hotel room; after leaving him at the World Series, he then saw me wake up at 3 in the morning to pop pills.

"Darren?" John asked. "Are you setting an alarm to take pills in the middle of the night?"

I tried to make up some lie, but I was too tired and the withdrawals were coming on.

I heard him ask me in the dark, "Do you think you have a problem?"

When you're partying in your twenties, no one notices because everyone parties in their twenties. When you are still partying in your thirties, people begin to notice. Your friends have gotten married. They have kids. They do not set an alarm in the middle of the night to pop some Vicodin. If you do, someone is eventually going to notice.

I didn't know how I was going to quit. How could I run a business without my pills? Plus, every time I did try to cut back I just got sick.

I figured that maybe if I tried to settle down, things would get better. Symone and I began to get more serious. I invited her to move in with me. The only problem was that now I was not only addicted to pills; I was also having to hide it from someone who was around all the time.

By that point, the pills had stopped working altogether. I didn't feel anything when I took them, which made me only take more. Then, I would take too many and get sick, throwing up first thing in the morning, on planes, in the back of limos.

I was a mess.

By the end of 2004, I found myself in Australia with Symone to meet her family. We were drinking the Australian beer, Victoria Bitter, and I couldn't keep my eyes open. I kept nodding off in front of Symone's family. I would fall asleep at the dinner table. She kept trying to make up excuses: I was working so hard; I was on antibiotics.

It wasn't antibiotics. I was taking anti-depressants, anti-anxiety medication, mood stabilizers, and painkillers. I had never been more depressed, anxious, unstable, or in so much pain in my life.

Then in 2005, Dennis began drinking again, too. The two of us together were a real pair. I had spiraled past functioning. Though my guys were helping to hold the business together, I was falling apart.

I remember being out with Dennis one night in London. We were at a strip club, and at the end of the night I put down my card to pay. It wasn't until the next morning that I realized I had spent close to $10,000. When I asked Dennis about it, he told me that I had insisted.

Another time, I came to in the morning with Dennis shaking me awake.

"We got to go, man," he shouted. "We're gonna miss the flight."

Even now, Dennis and I laugh about it because you know it's bad when Dennis Rodman is the one making sure you don't miss your flight.

My routine for more than two decades was no longer working for me. I was beginning to realize that I needed to make a drastic change. For the first time, I was starting to accept that I had to quit.

I just had no clue how to do it.

Chapter Nine

THE BEGINNING OF THE END

ADDICTION HAD BEGUN TO FEEL LIKE ONE OF those old cartoons where someone is tied to the railroad tracks, they can see the train coming, and there is nothing they can do to stop it.

I wanted out. I didn't want to wake up every morning, feeling like I wanted to die. Trouble was that out of all the deals I had negotiated in my life, none was more iron clad than the one that bound me to addiction.

More people were beginning to notice, too.

For 20 years, I had been disguising my using. Now, it seemed like every week someone was beginning to ask me what was going on.

In 2005, I was on Donny Deutsch's talk show, *Big Idea*. I was high on Percocet, and I had drunk a bunch of sake. I could barely keep my eyes open.

After the show, my PR team called a crisis meeting. My publicist sat across from me at a conference room table overlooking New York City and asked me what I was on.

If ever there was a time where I could have come clean, that was it. They would have whisked me into rehab. It would have either happened in secret, or they would have helped spin a great story about how I was getting clean.

They wanted to help me, and they wanted to make sure that one of their clients didn't completely destroy his business.

Did I confess? Did I ask for help? No. I did what I had been doing for 20 years with increasing frequency. I lied.

Even though I knew I had a problem, I just couldn't accept that it had any effect on my business. I thought if anything, quitting the pills would be the biggest risk to my success. My business was fine, and anyone who was worried about that clearly hadn't met Darren Prince.

I told everyone I had just taken too many allergy pills, which was why I was so drowsy.

I guess they believed me. I mean, who knows, right? People will accept the easy excuses until you're ready to tell the truth because it's really hard to call someone a liar, especially when that person is paying you. That was the thing; over the years, I had more and more people on my payroll. They call it co-signing someone's bullshit, but it's hard not to co-sign when that person is signing your checks.

The denial also applied to my relationship.

That year, Symone convinced me to move to Los Angeles to be bi-coastal. We got an apartment in West Hollywood. Part of me hoped the change of scenery might also change my using. They call it pulling a geographic. In the words of Jon Kabat-Zinn, "Wherever you go, there you are."

I already had a Rolodex of prescribing doctors out in LA, so once we arrived I picked up right where I left off. Since I was paying the bills, I thought (like an asshole) that Symone should just be happy with the life I was giving her: the parties, the celebrities, the lifestyle.

I mean, why should she also expect that I should be able to get through dinner without passing out at the table? Why would she expect to have a boyfriend who didn't get up multiple times in the night to get high? What right did she have to ask me if I was okay? Of course I was okay. I was Darren Prince. Didn't she know who I was?

After a couple of years together, she did. She knew I was an addict.

That didn't stop us from getting married.

My friend and gossip guru, Richard Johnson, ran a headline about the proposal on "Page Six" of the *New York Post* before I even asked Symone to marry me. So, I got down on one knee and pulled out the newspaper.

She was confused until I told her to read it. It read, "Agent Darren Prince is proposing to his girlfriend Symone, this evening in New York City."

She loved it.

At the time, I thought it was the most romantic thing I could have ever done. Now when I think of it, I realize that I always had to do things like that. They always had to be loud, splashed across the headlines. I had to do everything on such a huge scale because inside I felt so small.

There I was. I had just gotten engaged, business was booming, and I was also about to get another world-famous client.

Growing up in the 1970s, there were three people you worshipped: Elvis, Ali, and Evel Knievel. Obviously, I never had the chance to work with Elvis, but in 2005 I signed another legend: Evel Knievel. No one captured the imagination of 1970s America like Evel. His televised motorcycle jumps, including his 1974 attempt to jump Snake River Canyon at Twin Falls, Idaho, are to this day still four of the 20 most-watched of ABC's *Wide World of Sports* events. Throughout his career, he broke 433 bones and multiple Guinness World Records.

At the time, I had been negotiating licensing deals for an online casino for slot machines that would feature my clients on different games. Online gambling was a new, lucrative, and still relatively unregulated business, and sales were through the roof.

Evel was as old school as you got and wanted me to fly out to his home in Butte, Montana to meet in person.

We spent a couple of days together. I loved him from the moment I met him.

It wasn't surprising that his previous few years had been filled with chronic pain, given the way he had been living. We joked about morphine lollipops and shared beers at his favorite hangouts in Butte. Once again, there I was, 35 years old, drinking beers with one of my childhood heroes.

I headed home high as a kite and not just on the pills, which rarely made me feel like that anymore. I had just signed Evel Knievel.

It seemed like the business opportunities just kept falling into my lap. Thanks to Mercedes Ganon, a representative who works with PMG, we also started working with Pound for Pound boxing king, Roy Jones, Jr., and later that year, the "Nature Boy" wrestler, Ric Flair. All the while, I was sinking deeper and deeper into my own personal hell.

To be honest, I don't really remember most of 2006.

Acceptance works at a slow burn. I knew that people were talking about my problem. It was like a news story that was about to break. The question was, who would be the first to do it?

My mom and dad had finally asked what was wrong, and I told them I was having some trouble with prescription pills.

Once again, I was able to use the business as the evidence of my abilities. If I could take care of that, then surely I could also take care of myself. I told them everything was under control. The problem wasn't that I was losing the business. The problem was that I had already lost myself.

Symone knew what was going on and kept trying to help me quit, but she didn't really know what to do. No one around me was an addict, and they didn't know how to help. They thought that all I had to do was quit. If it was that simple, I would have done it that weekend in Philadelphia with Joe Frazier and Muhammad Ali. I couldn't quit. That was the real problem.

By this point, Steve Simon had become a key player in my business, and I honestly don't know if the company would have survived that time without him. He kept the lights on when I was blacked out. He knew what was going on. He would hide pills from me. Then I would become sick from withdrawals, and he wouldn't know what to do except give them back so I would feel better.

He finally told me he was afraid I was going to die. He looked at me sadly and said, "I don't want to watch that happen."

One day I was on the phone with Magic. We had been working together for over 10 years. Magic had given me so much. Because of him, I had been able to launch my business. I had been able to build my client list. He wasn't just my client or my mentor. He had become like an older brother to me.

It had been a horrible month. My first dog, Tyson—the dog who brought me Joe Frazier—had died. My house had undergone a major flood. Then, the online gambling business, which I had been connecting with so many of my clients, took a major hit. President Bush passed down some harsh regulations on the industry, and like that a cash cow dried up. I told Magic all of this. He listened, offering empathy, but I could tell he knew something else was going on, something much bigger than the death of my dog or a business deal gone south.

"I've got a problem with pills, Earvin," I finally confessed.

"What do you mean?" he asked.

"Painkillers. It's like I can't do anything without them. I can't get out of bed. I can't go to work. I can't function without the pills."

Magic paused. "Man, you need to get a handle on that," he said. "Those other problems, they're not problems. They'll pass. But you do not want to mess around with those pills. I've seen what it can do to people. You need to get clean."

A couple months later, Symone and I went on vacation to the Bahamas, where we met up with Magic and Cookie and their kids. I was bloated and miserable, and Magic could tell something was off.

"Darren, you don't look good," he said. "You need to take care of yourself."

But I couldn't.

A few weeks later, I was with another one of my good friends, Robert Belcuore. It was Christmas, and after dinner Rob asked me what was wrong.

"I've never seen you look so bad, Prince," he told me. "What's going on?"

I couldn't keep the secret anymore. I told him everything. I was an addict; I had been hiding it; and I was miserable.

"There are times I don't want to live anymore," I told him. "I need help."

Then, I got the ultimate wake up call.

In 2007, I overdosed. I was in Las Vegas for the NBA All-Star Game. That night, Dennis was having a huge party at a strip club.

We had hooked up with Mark Cuban that year, and Dennis was doing a show with him on HD Net TV called *Geek to Freak*. On it, Dennis mentored nerdy guys and girls, showing them how to become badass rebels. We hadn't gotten Dennis back to the NBA, but with the help of people like Cuban, we were able to continue solidifying his brand and his post-career success.

I was excited for the party and happy to see Dennis back on top, but I was also really sick with bronchitis. So, I did what any good addict does. For $500, I called a doctor up to my room to get a prescription for painkillers and Tussionex, an opiate-based cough syrup, which tasted like pineapple. It was heaven in a bottle and took about three minutes to kick in.

After picking up the prescription, I called Symone at the hotel. I asked her to order some Red Bulls and vodka from room service.

When I returned to the room, I threw back a few drinks, swallowed a handful of pills, and took a few shots off the cough syrup.

Within minutes, I was on the floor, chest racing. I felt like I was going to die.

I looked up to the ceiling and prayed, "God, please don't take me right now."

I don't remember anything that happened after that.

Apparently, Symone called 911. I came to with EMTs around me, one of whom was sticking a needle into my arm and putting an oxygen mask on my face. Steve made it up to the room and walked in as the EMTs were standing over me. I saw the look of fear in his eyes. It was heartbreaking.

I never made it to the party that night. The next morning, I woke up and looked at myself in the mirror. My eyes were bright red, and I looked like I had aged 10 years.

Regardless of what I saw in the mirror, my denial was still wholly intact. Instead of facing reality, I thought, "What an idiot you are. Who mixes Red Bull with pills and cough syrup?"

Then, I took a handful of pills and a couple of shots of cough syrup. Albert Einstein has been credited with saying, "The definition of insanity is doing the same thing over and over again and expecting different results." The difference was that I wasn't expecting a different result. I knew exactly what I was going to get, and it was the only thing I knew how to do.

I was definitely in acceptance. I knew I was an addict. Knowing I was an addict and recovering from addiction were, however, two very different things. As they say in the 12-step fellowship, "Self-knowledge avails us nothing."

When I got home, I told my mom everything. As close as I was to my father, I had always been a mama's boy. I remember being embarrassed by her affection when I was a kid, but as I grew older I wouldn't have it any other way. My mom adores me.

When she heard what had happened, she freaked out like any mother would.

She was also determined to fix it. She found an addiction specialist, and as soon as I got back to New Jersey, I met with him. He told me I was opiate addict and put me on Suboxone, which is an opiate blocker.

So there I was, on Suboxone, an anti-depressant, an anti-anxiety pill, and a mood stabilizer. It didn't help that I was also drinking multiple times a week to the point of blackout. I was basically living on another planet.

What had been living to use had become using to live.

I discovered a routine that worked relatively well. If I stopped the Suboxone for 12 hours, I could get up in the middle of the night, chop up some pills, and snort them. I would work for a little while and then black back out. I didn't want to be alive.

Then, I got married.

Even now, when I look at the video of my wedding, I feel sick. I can just see the addiction all over me. I looked like a wax figure, pale and sweaty. It was supposed to be the most magical weekend of my life, and I was miserable.

All of my closest friends were there. Magic, Dennis, and Smokin' Joe were in my wedding party. Magic gave a speech, and everyone was so happy for Symone and me.

Through Dennis, I was able to hire the band Boogie Nights for the wedding. Dennis, Magic, and Joe all got on stage with the band for a jam session. I thought to myself, "After all the bullshit Dennis has put me through, he might have just made up for it."

Smokin' Joe performed "Mustang Sally," and the place went wild.

By the next day, the honeymoon was already over.

The plan was that we would have brunch in New Jersey, and then I would take everyone into the city for a day of sightseeing and shopping. I had been detoxing for two days before the wedding and couldn't wait to get high again. I made it to the brunch, but I had already started using that morning. Symone knew, and the look of hurt on her face spelled the future of our marriage. I told everyone I just needed to run back to my condo to get a few things, and then we would leave for New York.

I didn't return. I went home and swallowed and snorted some more pills to the point of passing out. I woke up hours later in the afternoon with Symone and her family standing over me, furious.

Not only did I ruin the day for everyone; the façade was gone. Symone's whole family knew something was wrong with me.

If 2006 was a blur, then 2007 was a blackout.

One thing I do remember was my last conversation with Evel Knievel. It was the summer of 2007. Evel had always been known to be a tough SOB, but in his later years he became a born-again Christian, which I think softened him a bit.

On the call, he told me, "I think the world of you, and I appreciate how hard you've worked for me."

He congratulated me on my wedding, and in true Evel fashion he added, "I don't want to be a downer, but marriage doesn't last. You're gonna think about all that money that you blew."

It wasn't what people typically said to you after just getting married, but there was nothing typical about Evel Knievel.

I thought then—and realized as much even later—that I had paid for the memories and not the wedding.

He wished me a great marriage and a great life.

That would be the last time we ever spoke.

A few days later, Steve told me that there was a report online that Evel had passed away. I called his wife Krystal and found out that it was true.

I was heartbroken. In a short time Evel had become one of my closest clients, and I had never lost a client before. Symone and I booked the flight to Montana. I tried to start the Suboxone again, but by the time we made it to the funeral I was back to chewing Percocet's.

I remembered meeting Matthew McConaughey at the funeral. He was supposed to play Evel in an upcoming film and had called our office to ask about the funeral arrangements. I told McConaughey I was going with Smokin' Joe and that we would find him at the memorial.

I always had a way with celebrities. Just like that night at the Mondrian with Kobe Bryant, there was this instant connection. I was able to shine around them but in a way that never took away from their own glory. Pills had given me this superhero confidence, but now all of that was lost.

I greeted McConaughey, but it was an empty hello. I used whatever gas was left in my tank, but it wasn't what it used to be. I couldn't turn it on anymore. My mojo was fading.

Symone and I flew home in silence. Evel was dead, but it felt like so much more was ending. I just couldn't do it anymore. I thought as we flew back to New Jersey that Symone would be better off if I was dead. There would be insurance money for her. Steve, Nicky C., and my family could take the business.

I had tried going to a doctor. I had tried to fix the problem, and the only result was that I had gotten more sick.

I was in total acceptance of my condition, and I knew that there was only one way out.

I wasn't sure how I was going to do it, but I decided that I would kill myself.

The only problem was that I didn't have the balls to do it

Part Four

ATTITUDE
ADJUSTMENT

*If you want to change attitudes, start with a change in behavior.
In other words, begin to act the part, as well as you can, of
the person you would rather be, the person you most want to
become. Gradually, the old, fearful person will fade away.*

William Glasser

Chapter Ten

MORE IS REVEALED

By the time November 2007 rolled around, it seemed like more and more people were worried about me.

An even bigger issue, however, was how many people didn't even know what was going on. I think if I had bottomed out in public or been busted by the cops, it might have been easier for me to accept that I had a problem. I had gotten so good at living a double life, even my own sister didn't realize I was an addict.

The best thing I did was to start telling people what was going on. I just couldn't keep the secret anymore. It was killing me, but I was still alive.

That fall, I went to Indianapolis for the Colts-Chargers playoff with my friend, Frosty. Frosty and I went back 15 years. He had seen every big move and every low point of my life. Frosty and I were both die-hard Chargers fans and were stoked to go to the playoffs together.

The night before the game, we went out to a steak dinner. He had that same look on his face as my friend Robert Belcuore had had during our Christmas conversation.

"You don't look good," he told me. "What's wrong, bro?"

And just like with Rob, I told him.

"I don't want to live this way anymore," I told him, as I downed another drink.

"It sounds like you need to get help, man. You might need to get sober."

The thing was, I didn't know what getting sober meant. I was on Suboxone, which had been prescribed by an addiction specialist, and I had never been more miserable.

I was connected to every major celebrity in the world. I could get a front-page headline with a couple of calls. I had a Rolodex crammed full of contact information for major CEOS, future presidents (i.e. Mr. Trump), and Wall Street high rollers. I had the people who loved me: my wife, my family, my friends, and my clients.

And I didn't know how to get sober.

Whenever I hear about the opioid crisis today, I think about how hard it is for all of us. How can some kid in a small town with parents who work too much, friends who party too much, and teachers who either don't know or don't care, get sober when I couldn't?

Sure, we've all heard of AA or NA or rehab, but knowing about 12-step programs or having the money to go to rehab is not the same thing as finding recovery.

I didn't understand how sobriety worked. I had tried to quit and failed. Failure was all I had ever known when it came to quitting drugs. I kept trying, though. Symone and I agreed to have a sober dinner every couple of nights. As soon as I got back home, however, I would start chewing on pills to get rid of the pain.

That year, Symone and I moved back to the east coast. At Symone's request, we had gotten an apartment in New York. LA had seemed like a fun adventure compared with living in New York. I knew New York. I liked to party and do business there, but I didn't want to live there. I hated it, which had only added to the resentment building in our relationship.

Those sober dinners made it worse.

Do you know what it's like having to sit through dinner, waiting for the moment when it is finally over so you can indulge your 20-year love affair? Every dinner, I felt like I was being held in a vice grip with relief just out of reach. After one dinner, I looked down and realized I had been holding the wood table so tight I had dug a hole in it.

Things were no better at work. I did a reverse commute from New York to New Jersey. Every morning, Steve would pick me up at the PATH train. By the time we arrived in New Jersey, I would be passed out. Steve would drive me to work while I stared blankly out the window, nodding off. Instead of the office, he would take me to my old condo in New Jersey, which I had kept. I would go upstairs to my bedroom and pass out.

Steve didn't know what to do anymore. I had accomplished so much, yet I was wasting away in front of him.

I would ask Steve to hide the pills, and then I would start begging him to tell me where they were.

I started keeping prescriptions in a safety deposit box at the local bank. I would go into the bank early just so I could get to the pills. That way, no one could take them from me. The anxiety only got worse. I started having panic attacks. One afternoon, I had Steve take me to the hospital three different times because I thought I was having a heart attack.

I never checked in. I took a few Xanax and went home in the afternoon and slept it off.

I would take Xanax to calm myself down, mixing a fatal combination of cocktails on a daily basis. That year, Heath Ledger died from a mixture that resembled my daily recipe.

Months after Symone and I were married, we finally went on our honeymoon. We had planned to spend 10 days in St. Maarten and Anguilla. I left the pills at home, determined to be sober on my honeymoon. I thought it was the least I could do for my new bride, who I had already put through so much.

By the second day, I was in a fetal position on the bed. I had devolved into a hallucinating, sweating, shaking Zombie with diarrhea. Symone didn't know what to do. I did the only thing

I could think of. I called my dad and told him I was dying from pain. I had him FedEx me my pills.

Once I had them in hand, I could finally leave the room, but the trip was already wrecked.

Life continued like this for another few months. I don't even know how I survived. I was in a complete downward spiral. Steve did everything he could to cover for me, and I felt horrible for putting him in that position. Symone was trying to help me. She would give me massages, cook the things I liked. But I couldn't stop. Then, I got a call from my mom.

Her brother, my uncle Stewart, and his girlfriend, Andrea, were in town. Uncle Stewart was like a second father to me. As opposed to my serious, responsible dad, my uncle Stew was who I wanted to be when I grew up. He made a lot of money, blew a lot of money, and always seemed to have a good time doing it. He looked like Neil Diamond and always had the hottest women. Back in the seventies, he would wear polyester button downs with the buttons down low. My friends and I idolized him. I knew he had struggled with drugs before, but we never really talked about that kind of thing in my family. It's why my parents, even after FedExing me painkillers to Anguilla, still didn't know how to acknowledge that I had a real problem.

I met my uncle and Andrea at my old condo in New Jersey.

I don't think that day was any different than the one before. I hadn't overdosed the night before or done anything stupid. I was just done.

We sat at my kitchen table and talked. Andrea, who I had never met before, took one look at me and asked, "Are you okay?"

I had been asked that almost every day from the people who knew and loved me best, and I could never be honest with them. There was something about how Andrea asked the question that suddenly made me want to give a true answer.

I told her everything. I told her about every pill I was taking—the Suboxone, the sleep aids, the anti-depressants, and the Xanax.

After she heard my long list of pharmaceuticals, she smiled gently and said, "The Suboxone is the first thing we need to get you off of."

"I don't have time for rehab," I explained, even after divulging my sob story of misery. I told her I was a super busy guy.

In response, she told me her story. Both she and my uncle were sober. Andrea was close to five years clean at that time.

"You can be, too," she told me with a smile just warm enough for me to believe her.

She asked me, "Do you realize that you have a disease? That you are an addict, and your life has become unmanageable? Are you willing to do whatever you need to do to get sober?"

"Yes, I am," I told her.

Later that evening, we went out to dinner at Docks Grill in New York. Symone and my parents joined us. Andrea told me to bring my Suboxone to the restaurant.

When I got there, she asked me to come to the bathroom with her. We went to the stall. She took the Suboxone and counted out 10 pills, setting them aside. She put the rest in my hand, and said, "Now, it's time for a funeral. Flush them."

I flushed them, and I remember feeling a sense of relief.

"Better?"

I nodded weakly.

"Good. I'm going to manage the rest of these. I'll go over with Symone how she should give them to you, so you can detox off of them. You can't get sober until you get off the Suboxone. Do you understand?"

I did. Nothing had wrecked me like that so-called solution. Suboxone might work for some people but it just made my exit strategy take that much longer.

I wanted to be done with my addiction, and I didn't have that much time left.

The next day, I went to Puerto Rico with Symone for the weekend. Again, another island vacation where I tried to kick pills. Talk about insanity. I drank through much of the vacation, which we ended early, returning home on the third day.

I was trying to detox off the Suboxone, and I was miserable.

When I got back, I had to fly to Tampa with Nicky C. to see Hulk for some business. At that point, I explained to Nicky what I was on and what I was doing. He held me in such high regard; I had never wanted him to look at me any different.

The amazing thing was that he never really saw there was a problem. That was how good I was at hiding it.

I came home the next day. I had made it five days. Then, I totally lost my shit.

I got back from the gym and was about to call one of my doctors. I wanted a refill of Percocet. Miraculously, I called Andrea and my uncle instead.

I started screaming, "My brain is fucked, and I am opiate deficient. I need my opiates!"

That's when Uncle Stew grabbed the phone out of Andrea's hand.

"Stop lying," he yelled at me over the phone. "The disease owns you! Now, stop whining and get to a 12-step meeting. Put your hand up, and tell them you've got five days clean and you need help."

I hung up the phone and said, "No frickin' way." I went into the bathroom and opened the medicine cabinet. At least I still had Klonopin, which Andrea let me take for the withdrawals.

I opened up the bottle to shake out some pills, and out came two Vicodin. I stared at them in my hand like they were a gift from God. I must have hidden them in the bottle and not even realized it. Suddenly, that gift from God felt more like a curse from the devil.

I fell to my knees, shaking and trembling. I cried out, "I can't do this anymore. I need your help."

And that's when the miracle happened.

I heard a voice over my shoulder. Not kidding. I even looked around, thinking someone was there.

And the voice said, as clear as day, "I got you, and you're ready."

I'm not the first person to have that moment, and I'm certainly not the last. Maybe it's God; maybe it's our conscience; but suddenly we hear the Universe tell us we can do it, and we believe that voice. In that moment, it's the only thing we can believe.

I looked down at my right hand. The pills were sitting there. I was still on my knees. Then, in slow motion, I stood up and watched as I opened my hand, dropped the pills into the toilet bowl, and flushed them down. It felt like I was watching a movie of someone else doing it. It didn't feel real.

I was throwing away my more than 20-year love affair. Though I didn't know it at the time, I was about to change my life forever.

I walked out of the bathroom and to my computer. I found a 12-step meeting in my neighborhood that started in an hour. I asked Symone if she would come with me.

As we rode in the cab, I looked out at Manhattan. I realized that it was the first time in my life that I had wanted to stay sober more than I wanted to get high.

I walked into the basement of the church, and I introduced myself as a newcomer.

It was a Sunday night, and the meeting was packed. I had been to meetings before, but I could never hear them. It was like the words had always been muffled. That night, I could hear them clear as day. There were over 150 people in the room, and I felt like I knew all of them. For the first time in my life, I got it.

I felt a warmth and an acceptance I had never experienced in my life before. I felt like I belonged in a way I had never felt in my life. Symone decided to leave the meeting, but I stayed. For the first time since realizing I had a problem with pills, I felt hope.

I understood that it wasn't about changing overnight. It was about taking the first step towards change. I found out later this is what they call an attitude adjustment. Adjustments are slow. They're measured, and they don't happen overnight. If we take the time and practice with enough consistency, they lead to transformation.

I listened to everyone's stories that night, and I identified with every word. By the end of that first meeting, I knew I was a part of something bigger than me.

I heard the phrase, "90 meetings in 90 days." I heard, "Keep coming back." I heard, "It's a lot easier to stay sober then to get sober."

It was July 2, 2008. I stayed sober.

Over the next year, I threw myself into the 12-step program. I felt like I was back in high school, but this time I knew who I was. I found confidence in the rooms. I found love. I found faith. I also found out I would never graduate. Recovery was a lifelong process, but for someone whose life was about to end that sounded like an incredible gift.

I began to connect with people in ways I never had before. Sure, some of them knew what I did and it was exciting for them to hear my stories. For once, however, I wasn't trying to prove how cool I was.

Instead, I began to develop real friendships in the "rooms," as they're called. I heard stories that put my life to shame. I was struggling with luxury problems, but the people I met were facing far worse consequences—homelessness, prison—and they had come from far worse childhoods. Some had families like mine, but many more came from abuse and addiction. None of this mattered once we stepped foot into that church basement. We were all there for the same reason; we were all recovering from the same disease.

In those rooms, I was earning people's respect not because of my career but because of what I was doing. I was putting one foot in front of the other.

I couldn't help but remember the hope of my old therapist, Rhoda Gold, who had passed away a few years before. I was finding my purpose, not through cars or cash or celebrities but in my own self. Over time and with practice, everything began to shift.

I began to see my success not as some overwhelming gift that had been given to the wrong person but as an amazing opportunity. I had the opportunity to work with legends. I helped them to establish their post-career legacies.

Once the sport was over, it was my job to create the opportunities for my clients to be successful. I had done that for some of the biggest athletes and celebrities in the world. For the first time in over 20 years, I could own my own achievements.

In fact, I now felt them in the deepest parts of my soul.

As I worked to focus on my sobriety, I knew there was one client from whom I needed a break.

I called Dennis up and told him I had been sober for 30 days. He congratulated me immediately.

"I'm so happy for you, brother," he gushed.

"Thanks, Dennis," I continued, my voice cracking a bit as I spoke. "I think I need to step back for a little while. Steve will handle all your business needs, but I just need to focus on me for a bit."

I thought he would be mad, but if anyone could understand, it was Dennis. "No man. You need to get away from it all. The pills, the partying, all this shit. Get better, Darren. Get your mind right for you and your family."

Dennis moved down to Florida and started working with another road manager, Aston Bright. We all called him AJ, and he was an amazing guy. In a way, he was as big of a gift to me as he was to Dennis. I knew I was leaving him in good hands.

About a month and a half into my sobriety, I met the man who would change my life forever: Stephen Della Valle. Steve was a tough guy from Newark, New Jersey, who had been to prison and found recovery over 27 years ago. He had even written an amazing book about it called *Rising Above the Influence.*

In the rooms, he was a spiritual giant, and he became my sponsor. He told me that I had to put the same effort into my sobriety that I had into my using.

My travel schedule looked no different from before I got sober. Steve told me that if I wanted to stay sober, I needed to hit meetings on the road as though I was at home. This was one of the most important lessons I learned from my earliest days in the program. There were meetings all over the world, and I could find one wherever I travelled.

On my 80th day of sobriety, I landed in Chicago. It was freezing out. I called Steve, and he asked me if I was going to a meeting. I told him it was too cold out, and I would just wait to get home.

"Let me ask you," Steve replied. "If there was a strip club or a pharmacy down the street, would you walk a few blocks to get what you wanted?"

I told him, "Absolutely."

He said, "Well then, you need to put that same energy into your recovery. You travel more than anyone, and those road meetings are going to be your lifeline. You'll inspire everyone back in the meetings in New Jersey when you tell them about your meetings on the road."

I learned that wherever I went, I would always find a home in a church basement or the rec room of a community center. Montreal, Monaco, Anguilla, Turks and Caicos, London, Sydney, Fiji, Chicago—I've been to meetings all over the world.

What I found was that no matter what language we spoke, where we came from, or who we were, we were all united. We had all found the same solution to addiction.

After a while, it's less about staying away from the drink or the drug and more about connecting with people who understand you.

They call me Road Dog at my home meetings because I've probably hit more road meetings than anyone I've ever met.

I was two years sober when I found myself in Montreal and called a car service to take me to a 12-step clubhouse. When we got the meeting space, however, it was closed.

"You sober?" my driver asked in a thick French accent.

"Yeah," I told him. "I was trying to get to this meeting."

"I'm sober 25 years," he announced. "We can have a meeting here."

For the next 40 minutes, we drove around talking about life and recovery and what we do to stay sober.

As my sponsor Steve once told me, "It's not just about staying away from drinking and drugging. It's about the attitude adjustment. It's about becoming a selfless person, not a selfish one."

I began to realize that getting sober was a personal choice, but staying sober was a public responsibility. I had a voice and a platform, and I wanted to use my resources to help other people recover from addiction. I kept thinking that if it took me years to find out how to get sober, how could other people with far fewer resources and connections ever succeed?

My father was supportive of my recovery from the start, but my mother struggled with it. She was proud and relieved that I was sober, but did everyone need to know?

I knew it was hard. I also knew it was secrecy that kept so many addicts high and so many alcoholics drunk. There was no shame in addiction. As long as we continued to shame addicts, we would never be able to cure the crisis that had exploded across the country and around the world.

After a few years, my mom began to understand. In 2015, the New Jersey Mental Health Association honored me for Opiate Awareness Month. My mom realized that no one was saying, "Your son is a scumbag." Instead, she realized I had found my calling.

By that point, my uncle and Andrea had broken up. A year after I got sober, I was in Florida with my uncle, on our way to a meeting. He asked if Andrea and I talked, and I said we texted from time to time. My uncle said he wasn't thrilled with how the relationship ended, but he admitted, "She was one of the more special people in my life because what she did for you."

He was right. Andrea saved my life, and I knew that the only way I could repay that gift was to try to save others.

Chapter Eleven

AWAKENING

BY 2009, I WAS BACK IN BUSINESS. I HAD STARTED working directly with Dennis again, though our work no longer took place in the back rooms of strip clubs over bottles of vodka. I began to discover that removing booze allowed me to deepen my relationships with people even further.

As Dennis' road manager Thaer once said, "I don't like agents, but you're no agent." My ability to build real and lasting friendships with my clients was always at the heart of my success, but suddenly I was also able to be completely honest in those relationships.

Our client list only continued to grow. That year, we started to work with Scottie Pippen and Mickey Rourke, who was right in the middle of his awards season for *The Wrestler*.

In 2009, I got Dennis on *Celebrity Apprentice*. Since he'd won *Celebrity Mole*, I thought he would be the last one left in the boardroom. In one of the early episodes, however, Trump fired Dennis for being drunk on the show.

By that point, I had been sober for a year-and-a-half. I had watched from the inside, witnessing what drinking had done to Dennis's life. I didn't want alcohol to ruin this opportunity, too. I reached out to Trump's assistant, Rhona Graff, and I asked if I could speak with him personally.

Within hours, Trump called me back on my cell phone. I know our country is now divided over his presidency, but to me he was always a kind and consummate professional.

Trump asked me, "Darren, what's going on?"

I told him I had been trying to help Dennis, and I told him about my own sobriety. I asked if Dennis could at least meet with him before we left.

Trump told me it was really admirable for me to make that call.

"I had a brother die from alcoholism," he told me. "Ugly disease."

I told Trump not to tell Dennis I called. I wanted Dennis to feel like it was coming from Trump.

Trump said, "Why? I think it's terrific that you called, that you care about him. You sound more like a friend than an agent. I'm definitely gonna tell him that."

Who was I to argue with Donald Trump?

We got a call from Trump's producer the next day. They invited Dennis back for one final episode, where the players would be competing on a charity event. Dennis raised $30,000 for the charity, and his team ended up winning the challenge. Though

Dennis didn't stay on the show, he ended on a high note. This time, he had done right.

In 2009, I joined the board at Turning Point, a drug and alcohol rehab in Paterson, New Jersey. Through my work there, I began to give back to the recovery community. Steve Della Valle was also on the board, and I told him I would do what I could to help with their annual gala.

In the nine years that have passed since I joined the board, we have been able to bring many amazing people to the event, from Smokin' Joe Frazier to Vince Neil to Magic Johnson to Micky Ward and Dickie Eklund, the real-life boxing brothers whose story was showcased in the movie, *The Fighter*. Every year, we have raised hundreds of thousands of dollars to fund scholarships for people who need rehab but can't afford it.

In the last few years, I had also become good friends with a former Boston Celtic and well-known recovery advocate, Chris Herren, who joined us at the dinner in 2015. We were introduced in 2013 by a mutual friend, Jane Beup, who had worked with us to book Magic as the keynote guest speaker in 2011 for an event at the Hartford, Connecticut YMCA. Chris Herren is like the Michael Jordan of the recovery world, and he is as powerful off the court as he is on it. When we met, we discovered that we got sober 29 days apart. We have been brothers ever since.

Every year I have attended the gala, I witness another room of survivors. I see people like me who thought suicide was their only option.

The longer I have stayed sober, the more of a gift I realized I have been given. Not only was I released from drugs and alcohol; I also began to understand life in a completely different way. The things that used to be important to me—the cash, and cards, and playing the big man—just didn't mean anything anymore.

My attitude had been rightfully adjusted, and here was the craziest part: I had never been more grateful in my life. I wasn't just free from addiction. I had a whole new lease on life. It was like I was seeing the world for the first time. I could hear the birds singing. I noticed how green the trees were. I paused to watch the sunrise and sunset.

I also began to see the people around me more clearly than ever before.

I was becoming honest in all of my relationships, including my marriage.

Symone had been through so much of the mayhem; I thought that when I got sober we would be able to rebuild our marriage. I was wrong. I wanted it to work, but we had become more like good buddies than husband and wife. I just felt that we were both holding onto something that no longer existed.

In 2011, I filed for divorce.

I had become an action taker. I am not sure if Symone would have left, but I think that deep down she knew we weren't going to survive.

It wasn't easy. I had so much guilt around my marriage. Since getting sober, I had done everything I could to make the marriage work, and I began to realize that it wasn't anyone's fault that it didn't. I could finally let it go. Symone deserved to be happy. She deserved to fall in love and have a family of her own.

Then, I got the call. It was November 7, 2011. Joe Frazier had died.

He had been sick for most of the year. The month before, I had been with him at the hospital, holding his hand and laughing about playing blackjack with him while he told me about the nurses he liked.

"I like to chase the ones with the big asses." He laughed even as he lay in bed, hooked up to a million machines, dying from advanced liver cancer and Hepatitis C, which he had gotten back in his boxing days from all the blood and cutting.

It was such an incredible experience, to be there with him in the hospital. I was sober and present, rubbing his head and just being his brother. I was still doing the best I could to protect his legacy.

Lonnie Ali, Muhammad's wife, called when Joe was put into hospice and said that she and Muhammad wanted to visit him. I knew Joe wouldn't want Ali to see him like that, though.

"He's going," I told Lonnie. "I think he's past the point of visitors."

"Alright," Lonnie agreed, adding, "Let us know when the funeral is. We'll be the first ones on the plane."

When Joe passed, I was the Ali's liaison for the memorial. There were over 4,000 people there. The night Joe died, they had interrupted Monday Night Football—which happened to be in Philadelphia—to announce the news. The world had lost a legend; I had lost one of my closest friends.

I was standing there at the funeral in front of Muhammad and Lonnie, and I couldn't believe how much had changed in the nine years since the NBA All-Star Game in Philadelphia. I wasn't wondering why I was sitting there. I knew I had earned these friendships. They were mind-blowing, but they were also real and true. To an extent, we had all been awkward kids once, growing up in our little towns. These Supermen I had looked up to for all those years were really just mortals underneath it all, mortals I had gotten the chance to know and love.

Lonnie told me that she hadn't seen Muhammad so shaken since his mother passed. It was like watching his mortality right in front of him. The irony was that Smokin' Joe and I used to talk about going to Muhammad's funeral. No one thought Joe would go first.

In the end, they had both made peace with their pasts and were able to just be together as human beings. It was their legacies that were immortal.

I got Donald Trump, Mike Tyson, and Mickey Rourke to all give taped testimonials during the funeral. I knew Joe wouldn't care about the pomp and circumstance. He was the kind of person who treated everyone the same, whether they made $100 a week or $100 million a year. He wasn't a showman. He was just a really good man and one of the best boxers who ever lived.

Joe always used to say, "There's no wrong way to do right, and there's no right way to do wrong."

Though Smokin' Joe was known worldwide, he was always eclipsed by the larger persona of Muhammad Ali. During the memorial, Joe got the love and respect he always deserved. I knew he could feel it. I could sense his spirit in the air. I could hear him laughing and telling me, "Boss man, you really did it right this time."

I got through the entire funeral without a single thought of picking up a drug or a drink. Only four years earlier, I had been drugged out at Evel Knievel's funeral, completely unable to feel. So much had changed. I got to show up for Smokin' Joe as a sober, spiritual brother.

I received love and respect from the Frazier family, his business associates, and the boxing authority, and I didn't think it was undeserved. I knew what I had done for Joe. More importantly, I knew what he had done for me. I know how proud he would have been of me, knowing that I took care of Muhammad and Lonnie for him right to the end.

They say in the 12-step fellowship that we intuitively know how to handle things which used to baffle us. Our behaviors change, our attitudes change, and our ability to be present for everything—the good, the bad, and the ugly—changes the way we see the world and how the world sees us. As I walked out of the funeral and said goodbye to Lonnie and Muhammad, I knew what a different person I had become just by taking a few simple steps. I had put down the pills and found gratitude in its place.

Not long after Joe's passing, I was given another test. I was at the gym doing a routine with my trainer. I didn't realize until later that night that I had done something wrong. I was getting ready for bed when I looked down and saw what looked light a golf ball sticking out of my lower mid-section. Within a week, I had an appointment for hernia surgery.

It was my first real test with pharmaceuticals. I told the doctor that I couldn't take pain medication outside of what I was given at the hospital. I spoke with my sponsor Steve, who told me, "There's a difference between drug use and drug abuse."

I woke up from the procedure still under anesthesia. My best friend Jon came and picked me up. I sat in the passenger side of his car, staring out the window. I was definitely high, and I'll admit it felt good. By that point, however, I had many meetings in the spiritual bank; even the euphoria of the high couldn't make me want to give up the euphoria of my sober life.

I looked down at the prescription the doctor had given me. I had told him I was an addict, and I didn't want opiates.

Regardless, here in my hands was a prescription for 100 Vicodin.

I called my sponsor Steve from the car and told him the high felt amazing. I told him I was buzzed and that they gave me a prescription for Vicodin.

"Do you need them?" Steve asked.

"I'm in pain, but I don't want to feel like this. It's not me anymore."

"So, you'll be okay with Tylenol then?"

I told him I would be, and then I ripped up the prescription in the car right there. Jon was so proud.

The healing was brutal. I also had a catheter because of some bladder issues, but I knew getting high wasn't going to make it any better. I took Advil and Tylenol, and I got through it. The wildest part of the experience was seeing the shift that happened in my brain.

I squared up with addiction. I had the devil right in front of me, and I sent him a Joe Frazier left hook and knocked him out.

Guys from the program came to my house and brought me a meeting, and I was reminded again that as long as I was sober I could get through anything.

In the middle of everything going on with my health, I was dealing with a divorce that didn't look like it was ever going to end.

After it was all over, I could appreciate that Symone's lawyers were just doing their job. Our divorce was becoming more complicated than our marriage ever was.

Then, right when I thought I could see a light at the end of the tunnel, my accountant died. It was terribly sad, and his untimely death also threw a huge wrench into the proceedings.

I had to hire someone else, and Symone's attorneys made us go back to square one. I wanted to give her what was fair, but I also realized it was a four-year marriage with no children. There had to be some boundaries.

Again, the program came in. I was able to negotiate that horrible mess with as much grace as I could muster. I know I didn't behave perfectly at times, but I tried to be generous and understanding while also still holding to my truth.

PMG continued to succeed. We added Academy Award-nominated actors Burt Reynolds and Tom Berenger to our client list and continued to build the team. In 2013, Frank Basile, my old friend from the baseball card days, came to me and told me about this boy band that was getting big and that we should invest in them. I started working with their manager, a guy named Chris "Vo" Volo. The band had a lot of momentum and was booking some great venues. We thought we were getting behind the next big thing. Then, the media leveled off, and the band began to break up. The positive part of the experience was that through the investment, I began to work more with their road manager, Vo.

I asked Vo to come on board with us at PMG. He joined Steve, Nicky C., and me and quickly began to sign his own clients and broker deals.

We started working with more corporations who were interested in connecting with celebrities, and we started booking for them. We began pitching the company to the client and not just the client to the company. This shift changed everything. Instead of being one and done, we were able to start building relationships with other celebrities. We became a full-service marketing agency for both for the talent and the corporate side.

I was on top of my career again. I was committed to my sobriety.

As often happens in life, the best and worst were yet to come.

Chapter Twelve

LIVING IN THE PRESENT

IN 2013, WE GOT THE CALL THAT WOULD CHANGE Dennis' future—and maybe even the future of the world—forever. Vice Media reached out to us and told us that they wanted to bring Dennis Rodman to North Korea. They explained that there wasn't a lot of money on the table, but the exposure would be great.

At the time, Psy's "Gangnam Style" was all the rage, so I assumed they were talking about South Korea (I work in sports and entertainment, not world politics).

After a few months, we still hadn't received a contract and they kept changing the dates. I asked Vice what the problem was. They said there were just a lot of clearance issues.

"For Korea?" I asked.

After seven months, we finally got the contracts, and I took them over to Steve for review. He looked up at me in disbelief and said, "Dude, you cannot send Dennis Rodman to North Korea."

"Why not?" I told him. "Korea is all the rage this day. K-Pop…"

"That's South Korea, moron," Steve laughed. "North Korea is the dictatorship with Kim Jong-un."

He looked back down at the contracts and added, "I can't imagine why Dennis would go."

When I explained the situation to Dennis later, he was unfazed.

I told Dennis how the producer from Vice sent me a photo of Kim Jong-un wearing Dennis' '91 Bull jersey while the North Korean leader was in boarding school.

"All I know is the guy likes basketball," I offered.

"I want to meet him," Dennis told me. "Maybe me being there could open up some doors between him and President Obama."

The night before he left, the main producer at Vice Media called to make sure everything was going okay. I told him Dennis was ready and excited.

"This is going to be the biggest hit your client has ever seen," the producer told me. "I don't think you understand the magnitude of what is about to go down."

They were right. I didn't. I had never experienced anything like it. Social media was on the rise, and we had never seen anything like it before. It wasn't like the old days of Dennis' career. Now, everything he said and did had the opportunity to go viral.

As I discovered, that could be a really good or a really bad thing.

Dennis called me after he arrived. They had timed his visit to coincide with a goodwill tour from the Harlem Globetrotters, who had been scheduled to play for the North Korean leader and his guests.

Dennis told me that Kim Jung-un's top officials had debriefed him, told him how to address Jung-un, and said he would be sitting with him at the game the next day.

During Dennis' first visit, they treated him like royalty; during the game, he and Jung-un spoke through an interpreter about his time on the Bulls.

"Dude likes basketball," Dennis told me after. That was enough for Dennis.

I woke up five hours later to the iconic photo of Dennis sitting next to Kim Jong-un with Dennis applauding. That photo went viral with Dennis becoming the most trending celebrity on the planet.

I know a lot has been made of Dennis' trips to North Korea, but I think his visits prove the ability of sports to unite people no matter what they believe.

Dennis is aware of all the accusations against Kim Jong-un, but their connection wasn't about that. It was about basketball. Even still, when Dennis returned home the visit was all over the news.

Dennis had been riveted by his experience. He honestly believed that you don't grow a relationship with someone by alienating the person. He thought that if the United States government was willing to start a conversation, both countries would be better off.

When Dennis returned, I was contacted by the Irish online sports betting company, Paddy Power. At the time, it looked like there might be the first black Pope, and Paddy Power wanted to sponsor Dennis to go to Italy. Dennis sobered up for the trip. When he came back, he was offered another opportunity: a return trip to North Korea.

The next trip would not have occurred without a chance coincidence. Dennis had allowed me to auction off a game of HORSE with him at Turning Point's online auction. After the auction, the winner, a professor named Joseph Terwilliger who taught on North Korean culture four times a year, emailed and said that while he wasn't interested in the game of HORSE, he was interested in North Korea. We told him we were looking for someone to get us back.

We started talking to Paddy Power about Dennis going back to the country and bringing other basketball players with him for an exhibition game. Paddy Power agreed to sponsor a North Korean-American exhibition game, which Dennis would coordinate between the two countries.

Dennis returned to North Korea that September. Vo, who had become Dennis' manager after joining PMG when the boy band we were working with slowed down, went on that trip and was key in organizing the trips to North Korea.

For as much as people criticized Dennis for the visits, there was no doubt it was a career changer. Vice Media had been right. It was the biggest media hit of Dennis' life.

Afterwards, Dennis ended up being the only basketball player to ever open *Saturday Night Live*. Oprah did a special on him, and he started landing ad campaigns for Foot Locker and other companies. He also appeared on the cover of *Sports Illustrated*. He was a retired, 54-year old basketball player, and he was everywhere.

He was also obsessed with going back to North Korea.

Dennis returned to North Korea in December of 2013 to prepare for an exhibition game between American and North Korean basketball players, which had been scheduled for the following month. Dennis, Vo, and Professor Terwilliger helped put together the North Korean team.

Paddy Power had sponsored all of the previous trips. In December of 2013, criticism intensified over their support just as they were preparing to go public, and they had to back out as sponsors. They still upheld their financial commitment for the exhibition game trip scheduled in January 2014, even though their name wasn't publicly attached.

I went along for the January 2014 trip, though I had to fly in and out within two days. A lot had changed since we booked that first trip, when I had thought Dennis was going to South Korea. We were all aware of the gravity of what we were doing now. A lot of people might have thought it was all a publicity stunt. The truth was that after meeting and spending time with

Kim Jong-un, Dennis had genuinely developed a relationship with him and hoped he could build more good will through it.

We had heard stories about people who didn't come back. No doubt, everyone was nervous someone would say the wrong thing or do the wrong thing and end up in a North Korean prison. Not Dennis and Vo, though. They felt right at home in Pyongyang. On this trip, we also had a delegation of former NBA players organized again by Paddy Power to play an exhibition game for Kim Jong-un and members of the government.

We arrived in Pyongyang early in the morning. It was dark and freezing as we moved through customs. You could hear a pin drop.

The North Koreans treated us like royalty. I was driven through Pyongyang, which could have been a major city in South Korea with stores and business, people walking down the street. Everything was carefully planned and strictly monitored.

I made it to the Koryo Hotel just in time for another emergency.

I was checking into the hotel when I found out that Dennis' friend had made a dumb mistake by allowing Dennis to agree to do an interview with CNN while drunk.

I tried to convince Dennis not to do the interview, but some of the players on the US exhibition team were getting flack for going to North Korea and Dennis wanted to diffuse the situation. There was nothing I could do to stop him.

I was there, and I saw the taping, but I didn't think it was that bad.

Dennis was questioned about a Korean-American Evangelical minister named Kenneth Bae, who started operating a tourism company in 2012 called "Nations Tour," which offered Christian missionary trips into North Korean Special Economic Zones. That same year, it was discovered that he had been arrested and charged with espionage, and he had been in a labor camp since. When Dennis started making trips there in 2013, he had voiced his hope that Kim Jong-un would release Bae.

Then, Chris Cuomo asked the question Dennis wasn't expecting and Dennis sounded like he was attacking Bae.

After the interview, everything returned to relative "normal," or at least as normal as it gets for Americans travelling in North Korea.

The exhibition game was scheduled for the following day. We boarded a bus, which took us to a large military stadium. We watched a phenomenal routine from the North Korean military, all dressed in uniform colors, moving in perfect sync.

Everything in North Korea felt uniform. The clothes, the colors, the food, the manners; everything was organized and exacting.

The people were kind and warm, though, and they went wild as soon as they saw Kim Jong-un. When the North Korean leader entered the stadium, he was greeted with a 15-minute standing ovation that felt more like Beatlemania than a presidential appearance.

Dennis and Kim Jong-un sat together during the exhibition game, chatting and making jokes through an interpreter.

Later that night, I called Steve to tell him how amazing the game was.

He interrupted me. "You need to get home."

"What's going on?" I asked him.

"It's a mess. People are calling Dennis a traitor. He's going to be losing deals, and you could be losing clients. You better get back here if you want to save the company."

The CNN interview was a publicity nightmare. I was getting texts from clients, telling me Dennis had crossed the line. Dennis apologized days later, embarrassed by his drunken outburst. I told Dennis he had to go to rehab. The stakes were just too high.

He entered rehab a few days later when he returned to the United States.

Later that year in 2014, Kenneth Bae was released. He credited Dennis' rant for having helped his release because he made it possible for so many more people to learn about his plight.

Even at his worst, Dennis was a lightning rod. He drew people to him, and in this case it had led to the release of a political prisoner. It was basketball diplomacy, Dennis Rodman style.

Dennis and VO didn't go back to North Korea for another three years.

By the time 2015 rolled around, I was still trying to settle my never-ending divorce. The proceedings had taken three-and-a-half years—almost as long as we were married. I finally called in the big guns, hiring the same firm that Katie Holmes had used in her divorce from Tom Cruise.

It was like watching a Championship Finals match between two amazing teams. There were no winners, but at least it was coming to an end.

Symone had been the one to stand by me all those years as I tried and failed to get sober. She had wiped me down with compresses when I was sweating and shaking in bed. My sponsor told me to let the past make me better, not bitter, and I held tight to those words as I finally closed the book on that chapter of my life.

Just as one chapter closed, a new and exciting one began.

In March 2015, I met an Australian-Ecuadorian model named Priscilla (on Facebook, of all places). We had mutual friends and began chatting. She gave me her number and I called, she never got back to me. We would talk and make plans, and then she would give me the run around. Others might have given up, but there was something about her that made me keep trying.

She was living between Australia and Los Angeles and finally made the move to New York.

That's when I texted her one last time, telling myself that if she didn't write back I would give up. I decided to go bold on my last message, promising her, "Here's your chance to go on the last first date of your lifetime, especially now that you're 30 minutes from me."

Priscilla responded, "Good one. Let's go out when I get settled."

I took her to one of my favorite sushi spots in New York. Even though she told me I talked too much on our first date, I learned she was on a model visa in the US but also had her own web and app development company.

We were on our third website company at PMG, and I asked if she would be interested in giving us a bid.

As she began working in the office, she got to know the real me, and I got to know the real her. I know my colleagues were cautious until we got on the first conference call with this beautiful, extremely intelligent woman. They were awed by her tech-savvy conversation, not to mention her Australian accent. Her team designed PMG an awesome website, and Priscilla and I began to fall in love.

In some ways, my work had mellowed. In other ways, it had grown. I had learned the power of leverage early on in my career, and during these years I continued to use it to broker deals with Britney Spears, Jennifer Lopez, and Donald Trump. Oddly enough, it was all for collectible trading cards, the business where I'd gotten my start so many years ago.

A lot of A-list celebrities look down on autograph signings and trading cards, but I was able to show the value to Britney Spears' longtime manager, Larry Rudolph, who was also a friend of mine. I was able to sell the same concept to Trump's people who saw it as a tie-in with *Celebrity Apprentice*.

Once I had Trump and Britney on board, it wasn't hard to convince Jennifer Lopez's people, who saw it as a great opportunity to raise money for her charity.

Still, the art of the deal didn't give me the same high it used to.

I had gotten comfortable with the serenity of the sobriety. That didn't mean I worked fewer hours or any less meticulously for my clients, but my recovery had become my primary purpose.

I didn't just want to be sober; I wanted to help others achieve what had been given so freely to me, which is how I ended up being honored in 2015 by the New Jersey Mental Health Association.

Before the dinner, they released an announcement with a story about my work in recovery. Of course, this got my ego going. I had gone from Super Agent to Super Sober. Here's the thing about addiction, though. It will quickly humble you any time you forget about the consequences. A couple of days later, my friend Stacey Greene got a call from a man who wanted to buy tickets. His son John was struggling with addiction. As the man told Stacey, when John read my story it was the first time the father saw hope on his son's face.

They came to the event, and I met John. I could tell immediately that John was suffering. He had that dark, beaten look in his eyes. Once we started talking, I could feel that connection that happens when one addict talks to another. I had been where John was, and I gave him my number. Over the next several months, we stayed in touch. John would get one week of sobriety here and lose two weeks there.

One afternoon, I was at Le Montrose in West Hollywood when I texted John to see how he was doing. He responded that it had been really bad lately.

I wrote him back, "It's all good. You can go bad 99 more times; just get to me on the 100. I don't want to miss the magic when it happens."

I knew myself that it often takes 99 bad days to make it to that 100th one, the day where the door opens and the attitude begins to adjust. The best I could do was to be there for John when he walked through.

John recently celebrated his three-year sober anniversary, and I was there to celebrate with him and his family. He tells people it was that text that helped to get him sober.

Here's the blessing about sobriety: I have gotten so much more from everyone I have ever had the chance to help than they have gotten from me. Together, we keep each other sober, but we also get to change each other's lives.

For most of my life, I didn't believe I could perform without the cocktail or the prescription. I thought it was the pills and booze that gave me the magic. I thought that all of my relationships were centered on the party.

I'll admit that in the beginning of my sobriety, I had to learn to do a lot of things again. I had to find the balance between those old insecurities and my tendency to overcompensate. I work in a world where you win or lose by personality, and I had to rely on instinct since I didn't have any fancy degrees to back me up.

When you first get sober, those instincts are screwed up. It took me a few years to get back into the swing of what I was best at: building and maintaining authentic relationships with the people I had the opportunity to represent.

Here comes the shocker (probably not to you, but to me): those relationships became deeper, more authentic, and more honest than they ever had been when I was drinking and using.

This has been especially true when it comes to my biggest and most valuable clients. I learned early on in my recovery that whatever you put in front of your sobriety—work, relationships, money—you will lose. All of the people in my life know and understand that my recovery comes first. My clients, Priscilla, and my family are a very tight second.

In 2015, I reconnected with my old friend, the entertainment industry pioneer, Ryan Schinman. He was the first person to tell me that in order to be successful I needed to create a list of exclusive clients. Later, he helped my company to devise the plan for Dennis' brand and post-game career. He came back on board to look at my company's growth trajectory, and he noticed how laid back I was about life.

He joked, "You used to act like a king, but you're so mellow now."

I told him about my sobriety, and how it's allowed me to have faith in my business. Talk about attitude adjustment. I have learned that I can be the best for my clients without letting my work rule my life. Today, I have a life; for someone who only knew how to work and use, that is the biggest miracle of all.

Ryan started helping us find the holes in our business and begin building an epic team that could not only corner the market on talent but also corporate strategy.

In 2015, we found out just how powerful our clients could be.

For most of Hulk Hogan's career, he had maintained the perfect image. He was one of the most beloved figures in sports and entertainment. You couldn't go anywhere in the world without seeing fans swarm. People you would never expect would go up to Hulk and tell him how much he had meant to their lives. The fans meant as much to Hulk as well. He always made sure people could get in to see him, whether or not they could afford the cost of tickets.

As a Christian, Hogan was also deeply attached to his faith, an image that kept his fans close to him.

On July 24, 2015, I woke up in Miami to a stream of text messages: Would Hulk do this?

A sex tape had been leaked, but the worst part was what Hogan was saying on it. Within hours, he had been fired from the WWE, the empire he had helped build.

I knew Hulk wouldn't defend what he said any more than I would. I don't mean to justify what he said, but the truth was that he was going through a terrible time. He was in the middle of a divorce; he was drinking; and he had no idea he was being taped.

I flew to his house that day and told him I wasn't going anywhere; I would sleep on his front lawn if I had to. He was a man in need of a hug.

It's easy to crucify people. In the last couple of years this has happened to some folks who probably deserved it, but that doesn't mean the crucifixion isn't painful. Hogan had spent decades building his career, his image, his reputation, and a few bad words said at an even worse time were now going to destroy it all.

Even worse, he had no idea it was coming.

Most people would have rolled over, but Hogan was a fighter, in and out of the ring.

That day at his house, he said he would live in a cardboard box, fighting Gawker—the website that had posted the video—because of the stuff he had seen on their website. He knew he had made a mistake, but what these guys were doing was so much worse. They weren't just ruining celebrities but also everyday people. They were out to destroy people's lives.

He decided to go to battle, and sued Gawker, eventually putting the gossip site out of business. In the process, he also helped to change the privacy law game, which will likely have repercussions for how celebrity news is covered in the future.

I have had the blessing to know Hulk Hogan for almost 17 years, and I have known him to be tolerant, loving, and committed to helping people all over the world. I remember when it happened, his wife said, "God isn't doing this to you; he's doing this for you."

It wasn't easy, but I remained calm. I knew that all storms clear and that Hulk had never made a mistake like this. I knew it wouldn't last forever.

One of our longtime business partners was at 800-LOANMART, and they told us, "Look, we can't run the ads right now, but we'll sit tight with you guys."

It was partners like that who got us through until Hulk came out on the other side.

Just as one fighter emerged victorious, another fighter lost his battle. In June 2016, Muhammad Ali passed away. There was no way to explain that day. In some ways, I was happy that he was finally at peace. How much more could we expect from a man who had already given so much to the world? Still, I felt like a piece of history was over. There is no one else like him in the world today. There will never be another Ali.

Lonnie invited me to the memorial in Louisville, which was such an honor. Ali's hometown was filled to capacity. Almost 9000 people attended the funeral. Former president Bill Clinton and comedian Billy Crystal spoke, and President Obama issued a statement.

Like I had with Joe, I got to say goodbye sober. I was able to give my condolences to Harlan, Ali's marketing agent, who had done so much for my career and me. It was once again such a blessing to be there with the people who helped me become the person I was and to get to be sober and present for them. I shook hand after hand. I gave my love to his family. I was able to mourn the man who had changed my life more than 20 years earlier when I had booked him for my first signing.

I was able to make up for that night in Philadelphia when the hand of God reached out to me, and I popped another pill.

When I greeted Ali's family, they offered me nothing but love, and it reminded me that despite my years of using, I wasn't a bad person. I built these important relationships and did right by a lot of people, even when I couldn't do right by the people who loved me or myself.

The next month, I took another huge step. On my eight-year sober birthday, July 2, 2016, I proposed to Priscilla. This time, the proposal was a private affair.

We were in Aruba, and while we were at dinner I had the hotel staff decorate the room with candles and rose petals. Just as we were about to go upstairs, the manager said the room wasn't ready. I had to stall her in the lobby, which I think was a pretty clear giveaway that I was up to something. Finally, they said we could go to the room.

We walked in, and I could tell by the look on her face that she knew what was next. For me, it was exactly what I had always hoped that moment would be. I was sober and I was present, as I got down on one knee and said, "You make me the happiest guy in the world. Will you marry me?"

She was surprised, but she smiled. "Yes of course, I'll marry you, Darren."

We got back to New Jersey and celebrated with my parents. It was amazing for my Dad to see me so happy again. After so many years of struggling—before and after sobriety—I had found life again. I had found myself.

A few months later, we went to Anguilla—the sight of the honeymoon where I'd had my Dad FedEx me painkillers. This time, we lay on the beach and went to the gym. I even found an amazing couple from Maryland who owned some rehabs and opened up their home for 12-step meetings.

That January, my parents celebrated their 52nd wedding anniversary, an event I had attended every year since getting sober. Priscilla and I talked to my parents about the wedding. We both agreed we wanted something small and personal.

We all said goodbye. Though I will always remember that the food was terrible and no one liked the restaurant, the night couldn't have been better.

It was the last time I would see my father outside of a hospital room.

It was a couple of days before Trump's inauguration. Three days later, on January 13, 2017, I landed in LA. I had plans to go to my friend Joe Manganiello's birthday party with Dennis and Nicky C. When I landed and turned on my phone, I found urgent messages from my uncle. Then the phone rang. It was my uncle again. He told me I needed to call my mother right away.

"It's an emergency," he explained. "Your father has just been rushed to the hospital."

My mom was calm but clearly broken, as she explained that she had gone down to the basement where my father was working. He was hunched over in pain. By the time the ambulance had arrived, he had slipped into unconsciousness.

"They don't know if he's going to make it, Darren," she told me.

It was an abdominal aortic aneurysm. They had put him into an induced coma.

I took the first red eye flight that night while my sister, Vo, and Priscilla all sat with my mom throughout the night.

I called my sponsor, and he told me, "There is nothing you can do. This is life, Darren. You have a foundation that I haven't seen with people three times the amount of time you have. You're going to get through it. Your job is just to be of service to your family."

When I got back to New Jersey, the doctors told us he had a 15 percent chance of survival. He was all blown up with medications. He wasn't coming out of the coma. Over the next weeks, we moved in and out of my father's hospital room on rotation. Some days were hopeful; some were not.

After 15 days, the doctors suggested we take him off of life support. My mother and I agreed to meet at the hospital and explain to my father what we were going to need to do, hoping that he could hear us.

My mom stood on one side, and I stood on the other. We were talking to him, holding his hand, rubbing his arm, and then the magic happened. The machines went crazy, and the nurses ran in and told us to go outside and wait.

Ten minutes later, they came out and said, "He just broke the coma. You can go in and see him now."

Never doubt the power of prayer.

My old friend, Frank Basile, his girlfriend, Cindy, Priscilla, and my sister were with us. We were all crying even though we knew he was far from better.

When we walked into the room, my father was lying there with his eyes open. He was weak and could barely speak, but over the next 10 to 12 days, it was clear he could hear us. We were able to spend time with him, tell him how much we loved him. We got to say goodbye.

The day before he went into hospice, I went to visit him with Priscilla. Before we left, she said, "Why don't you spend some time alone with him?"

I went back that night. I held his hand, and I said, "Look, if God says you're going to be able to come back to us at 80 percent, then stick around. But if you're going to suffer, it's not fair to you. You can go. I'll take care of Mom. Go see Joe and Muhammad. Go home to grandma, and grandpa, and Uncle Joe, and let them know that I am okay. Let them know I've never been better. Mom will be fine. Just tell me what you want to do."

He turned away, and then he looked back at me. He whispered hoarsely, "I'm ready to die."

It was such a miracle. He shouldn't have made it out of that basement, but we all got to be with him to say goodbye.

I wouldn't be alive today without my father—not just because he made me but because of how he raised me. Everything good in this world I learned from my parents. I built so much of my success and so much of my career on the foundation of my father's faith in me.

I never needed a college degree; I went to Martin Prince University. I don't know that there was a better school out there.

I learned that in walking through the dark times sober, I was able to show other people that they could, too. I remember during that month, I spoke at a meeting and shared what I was going through. Afterwards, two guys came up to me. They were both in their early twenties and they were struggling. They told me that hearing me talk about walking sober through my father dying made them believe they could stay sober, too. It really was that simple.

I was in Tampa when my Dad passed away two days later. I had to go to Dallas the next day. While I was there, I drove to a meeting at the nearest clubhouse, a place called The Answer. I told everyone I had just lost my dad, and they understood. I had never met any of them before in my life, but they were my family. I wasn't at home, but I was right at home, and not once did I think of drinking or getting high.

When my Dad died, many people came to the memorial—clients, friends, and people from the 12-step rooms. They were all there to support my family and me.

Every day was an opportunity to adjust my attitude. I could have gone into a pity party, but I knew that other people needed me. It wasn't about me anymore; it was about what I could pack into the stream of life even when that stream felt like an overhead wave.

For eight-and-a-half years, my Dad had his sober son back, and what a blessing it had been.

Life without my dad hurt every day and still does, but at the same time I have been able to cope. Like my sponsor Steve had said, "This is life."

The next few months were a blur. Dennis went to North Korea again. Nicky C. brought on Charlie Sheen as a client. I decided to wait on a date for the wedding until my family had properly mourned. It felt like the months were flying by in a blur as I alternated between serene acceptance and heartbreak. I was learning to live without my dad, something I am still learning how to do.

Then, on July 2, 2017, I was reminded that he will always be with me. I was in Akron, Ohio for a corporate event with two of our clients from the *Caddyshack* movie. It was my nine-year sober birthday, and I didn't have any client meetings that day. The 12-step program was actually founded in Akron, and the house of one of the original founders, Dr. Bob, has since been turned into a museum about the fellowship. Since its start in 1935, over 150 12-step fellowships have evolved from their original concept, helping tens of millions of alcoholics and addicts to recover from a hopeless state of mind and body to live normal, healthy, spiritual lives.

I decided to make my pilgrimage. On the ride there, I spoke with my sponsor, my Uncle Stew, and another spiritual brother, my friend Dann in California. On each call, we talked about how amazing it was that five months after losing my father and on my nine-year sober anniversary, I was getting the chance to pay respect to the men who made it possible for me to show up sober during the most difficult loss of my life.

I walked up to the steps of the house when a man walked out.

He was tall, African-American, and if you squinted, he could have been a dead ringer for Smokin' Joe Frazier. To top it off, he was wearing a t-shirt that read simply, "Dad."

He walked out onto to the porch of the house, spread his arms wide, and called to me, "Welcome home, son!"

I burst into tears.

I think since I was seven years old, I just wanted to be welcomed home. I wanted to feel whole. I wanted to feel like I belonged. The journey took me a lot longer than expected. but my God what a journey it had been.

The people I have met, the people I have worked with, the people I will work with in the future...what I realized in that moment was that it didn't matter who you were, whether you were Smokin' Joe Frazier or an addict with three days sober in a church basement. You have the ability to change someone else's life.

They say to get self-esteem you need to do esteemable acts. I always thought I had to be rich, or handsome, or powerful to be confident. What I have realized is that all I have to be is kind. My father tried to teach me this lesson when I was five years old, but then again, I've always been a slow learner.

The biggest lesson of all is that I now know that I decide my future. Not just by the work I do, or the people I know, but in how I greet each day. It's my attitude that determines my success, and even more importantly, my ability to be present for it.

The lessons, and the clients, and the adventures keep coming. At least today I know that as I long as I aim high—without actually getting high—I will always make the shot.

(And if I miss, I've got Dennis Rodman, the world's greatest rebounder, on my team.)

ACKNOWLEDGEMENTS

BILL W. AND DR. BOB, THE TWO GODFATHERS OF the bridge back to life, the 12-step fellowship. Bill Wilson and Dr. Bob Smith started the spiritual program in Akron, Ohio on June 10, 1935. Since then, they have indirectly helped tens of millions of people around the world recover from alcoholism and addiction, become productive members of society, and live spiritual, peaceful, sober lives. I thank you both; without you, who knows where my life would be. One thing I know; this book would have never been written.

Adam Plotkin—thanks, pal, for the love and support over the years. It is always a pleasure doing business with you and your team as well. xo

AJ—Thanks for the love and support and determination over the years. Love you, bro!

Alan Elwood—Woody, can you believe it!? You were my right hand man at PMG when we started it all in 1995. We have created so many good memories over the years. Thanks for always being there when I needed you. Much love to you and your family.

Andrea Theodore—No words can explain the gift you gave to me on July 2, 2008. The only way I can ever repay you is by giving this gift of sobriety away to others. To say I love you is just not strong enough!

Anna David—Anna, you are a true beauty inside and out! We didn't just talk about my memoir; we made it happen. Now let's go save some lives by turning my darkest of days into the brightest of lights. #LightHustler, love you always. xoxo

Anthony Pitts and Larry Johnson—So much love for the two of you, I can't put it into words. Thank you for all you do and the love, support, and respect you have given my Dad and me over the years. The best to you both and your families for a lifetime of good health, happiness, and success. Love you guys!

Avi Levy—Thanks for the friendship and business relationship over the years, my friend. Looking forward to continued success together. Best to you and your family.

Bill Olderman—One of my brothers I have so much respect for. Thank you for showing me how to live an amazing life through all of its ups and downs. Most important, for showing me how to help others along the way.

Bill Watson "BW"—most importantly, thank you for all of our great personal talks about life and for supporting me on my spiritual journey. It's also been a pleasure getting to know your amazing family. Nothing but good health, happiness, and success to you all.

Brande Roderick—B, you are such a gift and such a winner at all you do with a HUGE heart. Thank you for trusting me over the years on some of our incredible business deals. Only the best in health, happiness, and continued success for you. Love always...

Brandon Steiner—Thanks for the love, support, and respect over the past 25 years, my friend. It's been great watching your success over the years!

Brian Gray—BG! Great working with you and your team and getting to know you over the past 10 years. Much love and respect and looking forward to a great future. Best to you and the family always.

Brian Geltzeiler—My man, we go back 35-plus years. I have always appreciated the love, support, and friendship. No matter who I was or where I was in life, you have treated me the same throughout. Didn't matter if I was in my early teenage years in camp, insecure and a bit shy, or spiritually broken 10-plus years ago, or spiritually intoxicated high on the mountaintop of life as I am today. You are a true definition of a real friend, my brother, never judging me or wanting anything in return; just to see me happy. Much love to you and your family. xo

Brian and Kevin Schwartz—Thanks for the love and support over the years, boys. Good things happen to good people, and you both and your families are on top of that list.

Brooke and Nick Hogan—My lil' brother and sister.... Thank you both for always supporting me on this journey. I am so proud of you two for the people you have become and the careers you have built. Only the best in lots of good health, happiness, and tremendous success. Love always, Chester xo

Bruce Rabiner—Brucy, baby! Thank you so much for your love and support and being there for me through life's ups and downs. Can't thank you enough, my friend. Best always. xoxo

Burt Reynolds/Todd Vittum—Burt and Todd, thank you for allowing me to be a part of your world. It has been an honor and privilege to work with you both and to call you friends.

Canada Bob/Mike Vettraino—CB, all I can say is thank you for the love and support and determination over the years. Love you, sweetheart!

Charlie Sheen—The Sheenius! A true treasure and a beautiful person, inside and out. I can't thank you enough for the trust and loyalty and our many personal talks about life. You deserve nothing but the best, always, my man! We have so much more to do together. Best to you, Jules, and the family. Love you!

Chevy and Jayni Chase—Chevy and Jayni, wow! Close to 25 years of working with you. More important has been the opportunity to get to know you both. It has been an honor and a blessing, and I can't thank you enough for allowing me to be a part of your inner circle, not to mention, trusting me at such a young age. And Dad soooo loved you guys. Much love to you both!

Chris Herren—My spiritual brother! One day at a time, you keep changing the game in recovery, my man. It is a blessing to know you and celebrate our sober birthdays 29 days apart each year. Thank you for always being there! I love you for life, bro! #ODAAT

Chris "VO" Volo—As my Dad used to say, "Vo was your best find ever!" He wasn't wrong. You are one of the best, my brother, and I can't ever thank you enough for what you do for G-Monster and me. You help me stay on my sober spiritual journey one day at a time, to be better, and to help others. Love you, my brother!

Chuck Zito—Baba, thanks for the loyalty and friendship over the years. So many great memories. xoxo

Cindy Morgan—Thank you, Cindy, for the great memories at all the *Caddyshack* events we've booked over the years. PMG thanks you for your trust and loyalty as well. Best to you always.

Corbin Bernsen—CB, thanks for all the laughs and the hard work. Appreciate the loyalty and respect over the years as well. Much love to you and Amanda. xoxo

Dan Schoenberg—Dan the Man. You're like the mailman and always deliver! I appreciate all you have done to take care of PMG clients and myself over the years. I am so glad we have become friends along the way. Best to you and your family.

Dann Rogers—BB, we came together three years ago for a reason. What a blessing to have you in my life. I am so proud to call you a friend and my big brother! xoxoxo

David Deutsch—My brother 4 life! We have seen and done it all together. I am beyond proud of you and the person you have become. Thunder buddies forever!

Andy Wayne, David Elwood, and Mark Schachter—Almost 40 years together, boys. I can't put into words what it has meant to me to see you be there for the new and improved DP over the last 10 years. You have shown me a love and respect I will never forget. Nothing better than our annual golf games and the fun we still make of each other, as that's what real friends do, lol. The best in heath, happiness, and success to you and the families. Xoxoxo

David Leb—Hey D, wow! What a run over the years. You are a true blessing in my life. All business aside, it's the fact that you are a friend to the end, which means more than any-thing. Love you, bro!

Dennis Rodman—DR, I write this with tears running down my face. Our love and respect for one another can't be put into words. You have taught me to stay true to myself and not listen to the haters and doubters. I get the honor of knowing the real you with that BIG, beautiful heart you have. You have also taught me so much and given me the confidence I needed to be, as you say, a "Super Agent." We have so much more to accomplish together, so let's go shock the world again and again! Love you bro, and proud to call you family.

Dominique Wilkins—Hey pal, such a pleasure getting to know you and work with you over the years. Looking forward to a continued, long, successful future, bro. xoxo

Dr. Lou Barretti—Lou, the best therapist out there, lol. Can you believe this? Ten years after we first met, I am writing a book? It may even help a few people, which is the real blessing and purpose of it all. Thank you for always being there and for helping to keep me on the right path. xoxo

Elliot Lovi—Elliot, you were the one teacher who believed in me growing up, and I will never ever forget it. I often hear some teachers really impact their students' lives, and you are on the top of that list for me! Only love to you and your family...

Eric Bischoff—EB, thanks for being you, pal. You are a great guy all around, and I wish you the best in life always.

Erik Kritzer—EK, thanks for all you do. It is a pleasure working with you side by side, and getting to be boys more than anything. Much love and respect always....

Eytan Sugarman—Hey Pal, although we don't get to see each other much, you know we are always cheering for one another. So great to watch your incredible, much deserved success, my brother. Nothing but love and respect for you. xoxo

Frank Basile—Yoooo, partner! Thirty-four years together. Can you believe it? You were there in the beginning, then when I fell, then when I got back up again, and you just kept pushing me forward until I got back on top. We have so much ahead of us, and I am so blessed for what we have done already. I certainly wouldn't be where I am today without you. Love You bro!!! Best to Cindy and the family. xoxo

Forrest Golembeske—Frumpy, a true friend is what you are and have always been. You have been there for me both when I was struggling and when I was on the top of my game. And you're my Chargers buddy for life, which is a big bonus! Love you pal...

Garrett Hade—Hey Garrett, you're a true blessing to the recovery community. What you continue to do to help save lives is amazing. All the best, my friend!

Gary Martin Zelman—My brother from another mother! Thank you, pal, for the love, support, and respect over the years. Nothing but love for you and your family. xoxo

Gary Vaynerchuk—Gary Vee, thanks for always taking the time to talk and meet with my clients and me. It is so great to see you continue to build your empire. Putting the mogul aside, you are a great guy who understands that life is about helping and inspiring others. Much love and respect!

George Triantafillo—Hey George, thank you for the love, support, and friendship over the years. You always come through when we need you, and are so appreciated for all the assistance with Dennis and other PMG clients. All the best, my man. xoxo

Greg Bruno—So many laughs and good times over the years, GB, from the early years of the baseball card days at Prince of Cards to the launch party for PMG. When you knew I had hit my lowest point in life and finally turned the corner, those laughs over sushi were just what I needed. Love you, POG Boy. Best to you and the family.

Greg Donner—Hey pal, it's hard to believe we only started our bromance 10-plus years ago, right around the time I started my spiritual sober journey. The one thing that has stayed consistent throughout all our ups and downs is the non-stop laughing. Thank you for the love and support always. As I like to say, real success is measured by how we all rise after we have fallen. Best in good health, happiness, and success to you and your beautiful kids.

Greg Williams—One of the all-time greats in the addiction recovery advocacy space! What a privilege to get to know you, bro. You have already accomplished so much on an epic level, helping to change and save lives. What's amazing is how much more is ahead. Best to you and the family always...

Harlan Werner—HJW, I can't put into words what you mean to me. You brought me into your inner circle when I was only 25 years old. We have been through so much together. I can never repay you for all the doors you opened for me, but what I can do is keep making you proud. It has been an honor and a blessing to be able to call you one of my true mentors, and you happen to be married to one of the best girls ever. xoxo to you, Christine, and baby Nicky.

Henry Holmes—King Henry! Wow. I can't put into words what you mean to me. You're not only an all-time legend in the entertainment industry; you're an even better person. You trusted me at such a young age and opened so many incredible doors for me. I am forever grateful. And it's a huge bonus that we're both die-hard Chargers fans! Love you, buddy....

Howard Stern —Thank you, Howard, for always giving PMG clients the platform to be themselves, have a good time, and promote what's important to them, as well as always having their backs. Our guys—Smokin' Joe, Dennis, Hulk, and Magic—have always had a fun time with you and your dream team (Robin, Gary, and others over the years).

Hulk Hogan—Immortal One! What an incredible blessing you have been to PMG, my family, and me. I can't thank you enough for the privilege of being able to say that I have been Hulk Hogan's sports agent for the last 17 years. Even more, it is really the man you are that just blows me away (and everyone else around you). You have inspired so many lives across the globe over the last 35 years. To call you a close friend is an even greater honor. Thank you for always being there for me and the boys. You and your family deserve nothing but the best in good health and happiness. Thank you, thank you, thank you. Best always to you, Jennifer, and your amazing kids. Love you for life!

Isiah Thomas—Hey Isiah, thank you for the friendship over the years and for all you do to look out for Dennis. We both appreciate it. You are first class all the way, a Hall of Famer off the court as much as you were on it.

Jason Binn—JB, we go back more than 25 years, and what great times we have had together! It has been a gift to see the mogul you have become, and thank you for always treating me like a friend. Here's to so many more great times ahead for us. Love you, pal!!!!!!!!!!!

Jason Koonce—Hey bro, in such a short time you have become family. Looking forward to so many more great times, more laughs together, and watching you grow to even more epic success professionally. All the best to you and your family.

Jeanie Buss—Jeanie, you are a true gem! I can't thank you enough for our friendship and for always, always being there. Such a special person who happens to be the most powerful and smartest woman in all of sports! An honor to call you a friend. Love always xo

Jeff Hamilton—Jeff, thank you for all that you have done to open doors for me and for believing in me at such a young age. Mom and Dad always loved you, too, and you will forever be a special part of the Prince family. All the best, always, my friend. Love you. xoxo

Jimmy "Amo" Amorosi—Nothing but laughs and great times over the years, kid! When you knew how broken and defeated I was and saw how I was hiding my secret addiction from the world, you never held back your feelings. It took me several years until I finally had my personal spiritual awakening, and I will never forget you being one of the first to tell me how proud you were when I went public with it all. Love you, Baba!

Jimmy "Mouth of the South" Hart—Jimbo, we can't thank you enough for all you do assisting us to make it easy. You are certainly one in a million. Keep on dancin'! Love ya, darlin'!

Joe Manganiello—Hey Joe, thanks again for being a friend and supporting me in my journey. You are a first-class guy who deserves all the blessings in life...Love and respect, my man!

Joe Tuttle—Hey bro, so glad we reconnected recently because you now see the best version of me versus 20 years ago. What you've built is incredible, as well as all the lives Banyan Treatment Centers have saved. Best always to you and your family.

Joey Gamberale—Hey Joe, thanks for the friendship over the years and for all the great memories we've had. Love always...

John Bakhshi—John B, my brother! Thanks bro for the love, support, and respect over the years. Continued success. You deserve it all, pal!

John Conklin and Joe Lupo—You are two great people I'm so happy to have met and worked with, thanks to our boy, Bruce. Thank you for the friendship as well. Wishing you guys a lifetime of good health, happiness, and continued success.

John Salley—Thanks bro for always looking out for Dennis and trying to assist me anyway you can over the years. You are a great guy who deserves the best always.

John Stampone—My spiritual brother, words can't express how proud I am of you, which is why I had to write about how we met in this book, lol. We walk this road together, side-by-side, one day at a time. Without a doubt, you have been one of the greatest gifts during my spiritual sober journey. You have helped me so much more than I can ever help you. Only the best in health, success, and happiness as you continue to give the gift away. Best always to your family as well, bro. xoxo

Jonathan Erde—My BFF, we go back 42 years, and what a run! So many great memories. Thank you for always treating me the same and keeping me grounded. Love you, baba ghanoush!

Jon Lazarus—Hey Big Jon, thanks so much for the love, support, and guidance over the years. Always so great having one of our talks about life and of course, sports. You are one of the real blessings in my life and truly a role model. Best to you and Gail and the rest of the family.

Jeff Rosenberg and Bobby Mintz—Almost 35 years of love and respect, my good friends! Doesn't happen often, especially considering how young we were. Proud to call you both true friends to the end and so happy to see the tremendous success you have had. Best always to you and your families.

Jill Leone and Larry Bird—Thank you both for trusting me enough to work with me back in 1995 and at such a young age. It was a true honor, especially being a life-long Boston Celtics fan. But business aside, it has meant more than anything to call you both friends. Only the best in health, happiness, and continued success!

Joe Montana—Hey pal, aka the GOAT! I can't thank you and Mikey enough for giving me the opportunity to work with you guys 22 years ago when I needed the support the most.

The real privilege has been getting to know you personally as a friend. My best always to you and your family.

Jules Feiler—JF, thanks for being a good friend over the years and for getting the best PR for my clients and me when it was needed! Love you, pal...

Kevin Freistat—KF, thank you for the love and support on my spiritual journey and for understanding who I am and the person I try to be one day at a time. The best in good health, happiness, and continued success, my friend.

Kevin Harrington—KH, thank you for the friendship and the privilege to work with you over the years. So excited to see what else we can create in the future! xoxo

Ken Goldin—Hey pal, wow, we go back 30 plus years, and I am honored to call you a real friend to the end. So happy for all your success. Best always to you and your family.

Kristen McGuiness—Thank you for doing a sensational job with me on this book. You literally deserve a big award for it and for putting up with me lol! xoxo

Kyle and Brittney Bell—Thank you both for the love and support over the years. You are beautiful people, inside and out. Wishing you and your two little princesses a lifetime of good health, happiness, and continued success. Love you both!

Kylin Furlow—My man Kylin, you inspire all of us every day. You never once said, "Why me?" but instead, "Try me, God!" You are a huge blessing in my life and part of team PMG forever, my good friend. Love you!!!

Larry Rudolph—Hey pal, thank you for the love and support over the years. It's also refreshing to see that you, like me, enjoy dressing super casual for the big business meetings. Lol. You can do whatever you want because you became an industry icon along the way, but it's the man you are and the friend I have in you that impresses me the most. Best always to you and the family.

Lonnie Ali—Lonnie, thank you and Harlan and Team Ali for the trust you and Muhammad placed in me at such a young age. I know we all miss him. The world is such a better place because of him; because of all you did while he was here; and because all of the work you continue to do while he is above looking down on us all. Xoxo

Lon Rosen—Hey Lon, thank you for allowing me to be a part of team Magic Johnson at 25 years old. I know very few people who can say that and appreciate you very much for your trust, support, and friendship. Best to you and the family always.

Matt Byars—Thanks, pal, for the friendship and loyalty over the years, as well as the effort you put into making things happen.

Micky Ward—Hey champ, thank you so much for being the person you are. I knew you were a first-class champion, as well as first-class person, the minute Nicky C. brought you to PMG. Thank you for all you do for us. Much love always....

Missy Levinson and family (Rich, Gail and Robyn) —For the past 28 years, you guys have been my second family and very, very special people in my life. Tough to put into words the love I have for all of you. Wishing you and your families nothing but the best in good health, happiness, and success.

Earvin "Magic" and Cookie Johnson—Once again, I sit here in tears. Earvin, you are my first boss, the man who took a chance on me and became Prince Marketing Group's first client. All I can say is THANK YOU! You never gave up on me and allowed me to be a small part of your tight inner circle, and for that I can never repay you. You believed in me and gave me wings and confidence. For the first time in my life, you made me believe, "I can do this!" That I am someone, and I am going to show the world I am here for a reason. I am so honored that you and Cookie are a part of my family. It has touched the Prince family so deeply, and I know my father is looking down with a huge smile and saying, "Earvin, father to father, thank you again for helping my son." May God continue to bless you, Cookie, your children, and the rest of the amazing Johnson family always! Love you forever and ever!!!!!!!!!!!!

Marion Deutsch and Becky—My other mom and sister! I love you both more than you know. You two are such special people in my life. xoxoxo

Mark Cuban—Hey pal, thanks again for always being so accessible to PMG and me. It's a rare quality for someone with the historic success you have had, and it also shows me why you are where you are. Thank you for always supporting and being a friend/fan to a few of our clients as well. All the best to you and the family and a lifetime of good health, happiness, and continued, epic success.

Molly Ann Bracigliano and Carmela Hladki—Two very special women who have always supported my spiritual sober journey. I can't thank you both enough for that. Wishing you two a lifetime of good health, happiness, and continued success. Love you both and the MAB team (Jared and Joey)!

Mom and Stacey—Mom, I don't have enough room on these pages to write about the love I have for you and how proud I am of the way you landed on your feet since Dad passed. And SJP, what a run we have been on as sister and brother. The laughing and memories will be in my heart forever. We have so much more to do. This is your time now to be a rock star, and I will be in the front row, cheering you on as Dad and Papa Joe look down! Love you both sooooo much.....

Michael "Berto" Bertolinni—Berto, words cannot express what you mean to me, and the chance you gave me working with you and Joe at a very dark time in my life. You never judged me, and I will never ever forget that. Love you bro, forever!

Mead Chasky—Thanks, my man, for always being a friend and supporting me in all I do. Best to you always....

Mercedes Ganon—Hey Merc, thanks so much for the love and support over the years and being my cheerleader. I am so proud of all you have accomplished and excited about our future projects. xoxo

Michael Okeefe—Hey pal, thanks for the love and support over the years. Been great working with you but better getting to know you as a real friend!

Michelle Rodman—Hey Mich, what a run we've had the past 15 years lol. Thank you for the love and support, and thank you for making those gorgeous babies, DJ and Trinity. Xoxo

Mike Osso—Hey pal, thanks for coming into my life when I needed you most. Only the best in health, happiness, and success for you and the family. xoxo

Mykl Howard—Happy to call you a friend, bro. Keep kicking ass and building that empire and family. lol

Natalie Wilson—Nat, you are one of a kind and a true blessing to me and so many others. You deserve the best in health, happiness, and success always, and you just happen to be the best celebrity gate keeper I've ever dealt with for Mr. J. I'll always be there if you ever need anything. Love you always. xoxo

Nicky C.—My brother, I am so very proud of you, and thank you for the love and support on my journey. You know Needle is looking down with a big smile on his face with all you have accomplished. Twenty years strong together and so much more ahead us. Love you. xoxoxo

Noah Teppeberg and Jason Strauss—Can't believe it's been almost 25 years, guys. Such a privilege to see your tremendous growth and success across the world. You deserve it all! Thank you for the love and respect to my clients and me over the years as well. xoxoxo

Patrick Ganino—Hey pal, thank you again for all the hard work you do behind the scenes to make PMG and me shine. We all appreciate what you do and the person you are as well. All the best to you and the family always!

President Donald J. Trump—Mr. President, thank you and your administration for the privilege of involving me in the Opioid Crisis Mission. I can only hope I am able to help educate and prevent youth from going down the same road I did, as well as give assistance to those who are already in the hell of opiate addiction. Thank you for always supporting our galas at the Turning Point Rehab and for being a fan and friend to many of our celebrity clients over the years.

Priscilla Caiza—One of the all-time most special women in my life. Priscilla, thank you for allowing and accepting me as me and supporting me on my mission and journey. And for your love of Rodney as well lol. I am always so grateful for your input and your view on anything I need assistance with. I am so excited for our future together and will do whatever I can to make you happy and proud. I love you. Xoxo, Egg Head!

Rabbi Peter Kasdan—Rabbi, you have been one of the most special people in my life for over 40 years. Only the best in health and happiness to you and Sheila and the kids. Love you both!

Ric Flair/Wendy Barlow—What a true blessing having both of you in my life. I am so honored by your love and respect and trust. Wendy, I love our spiritual talks and the way you look at life. Nothing but a lifetime of good health, happiness, and success to you both. Love you two very much.

Robert Belcuore—Duke, it seems like yesterday we met at six-years old at the stream behind your parents' house. Since day one, you have always been there, and we know that life isn't about how high you stand on the top of the mountain but how we rise after we have fallen. Here's to many more dinners (on me, of course)! Much love to you and your amazing family.

Roy Jones, Jr.—Hey Champ, thank you for the journey together and for giving PMG the opportunity to represent you. You are first-class all the way, in and outside of the ring. I am honored to call you a friend. Much love, bro. xoxo

Ryan Chisholm—Such a privilege to get to know you, bro. You are a real friend, and thank you for the love and support over the years. Can't wait to see what our future holds. I know we are going to be creating some epic projects together. Much love to you and the family. xoxo

Ryan Fiterman—Hey bro, thank you for the love, support, and respect over the years. Proud to call you a friend. Best to you and Kayla. xoxo

Ruben Martinez—My adopted Jewish brother lol. Thank you for the love and support over the years. Best to you and the family. xoxo

Ryan Hampton—My man and recovery game changer, keep saving lives and doing what you're doing! It's an honor to watch you take over the way you have been. A real blessing to have you in my life and call you a friend. Love you. xoxo

Ryan Schinman—Schindog, we go back to close to 28 years. To watch you become an industry pioneer was just incredible, but it's the man you are and the friend you have been that impresses me most. You are always there for me when I need you, and I can't thank you enough for that and what you do for PMG and our clients. Thank you to your amazing wife, Sam, as well for her love and support. The best to you and your three gorgeous kids. Love you forever!

Scooter Braun—Hey pal, such an honor to watch you continue to build your epic legacy. You are a once-in-a-generation type of guy who understands it's about giving back. You always respond when I reach out no matter how busy you are, which is exactly why you are where you are because you stay on top of everything. Much respect and lots of good health, happiness, and continued success to you and your family.

Scottie Pippen—Hey Scottie, thanks again for the assistance early on with Dennis. It's also been great working with you over the years as a PMG client. All the best to you and your family.

Steve Costello, Eric Levy, and Harlan Friedman—Some of the nicest, most loyal guys I know. Thank you for always supporting my spiritual sober journey and being there when I needed you. Nothing but love and respect for you three. xoxox

Stan Ross—Hey pal, I can't thank you enough for the love and support. You are truly one of a kind and deserve simply the best. Love to you and the family. xoxo

Stephen Della Valle—WOW! How do I put into words what you have meant to me? I simply can't, so I will just show you by my actions every day. You are my #1 spiritual brother. Without you, I don't think I would be alive today to write this book. So, thank you!!!!!!!!!!!!!!!!!! Love to you and your family. Xoxo

Steve Mills—Hey Steve, you are first class all the way! Though I miss seeing you around town, I know you're making all the moves to make my friends happy who are lifelong Knicks fans. Thanks for the support and friendship over the years. My best to you and the family!

Steve and Toby Rome—Thank you both for the love and support over the past 30 plus years. Two very special people in my life who deserve nothing but good health, happiness, and continued success. Much love to you and the family xoxo

Steven Simon—S2, what a run its been. Thirty-eight years together is a miracle...So proud of the work you do here at PMG but more impressed by the person you have become along the way. And thank you for the loyalty and love and support always. All the best always to you and Allison. Love you pal.

Symone Maree—Thank you for being there for me in my darkest days and watching me turn my life around. Best in health and happiness to you and your family.

Tim Ryan—Another bad boy recovery advocate, changing the game. Keep doing your thing my spiritual brother! We have such an amazing future together. Love you, bro!!!!!!!!

Thaer Mustafa—PUTZ, thank you for all that you do. Most important, for supporting me on my journey. You are one of a kind, and I will always appreciate our friendship and what you mean to me. Love always...

Uncle Stew—How else can I put into words what the most special man in my life means to me? I really can't! You are the other father figure in my life, and if it wasn't for you and our plan to meet on July 1, 2008, I know I wouldn't be alive and sober today. A nephew couldn't ask for a better uncle. I love you more than you will ever know. xoxox

Wendell "Big Will" Williams—Hey bro, thank you for all you do and our amazing spiritual talks. You are an amazing guy, and I appreciate the great friendship we have built. Wishing you only the best in life. Love you. xo

Warren Greene—Thank you for the love, support, and respect over the years, my friend. We're both so busy that we don't get to talk that much. But, you are the type of friend that, when we do reconnect, we can pick up right where we left off, as if no time has gone by. And we both see the world the same way. All the best to you always in all that you do. xoxo

Dad—I know you are not down here to read this book, but I know you don't need to be. Why? Because you lived it! Every moment you were there with me, through all of the ups and downs and in-betweens. You asked me years ago to write this to try to help people. Well, it has finally happened. I know you are looking down and smiling with Smokin' Joe. I miss him soooo much, too. Love you forever, Dad.

FURTHER THANKS

I COULD HAVE FILLED AN EVEN LARGER PORTION OF this book, thanking people who have helped, assisted, or impacted my life personally or professionally at one time or another over the past 40 years. For anyone who has worked with us at Prince Marketing Group, thank you sincerely for your support and trust. For those who have reached out to me in person, via text message or through my social media pages, I have appreciated each and every one. They've helped keep me on this spiritual sober journey one day at a time. From the bottom of my heart, thank you, thank you, thank you for the love, support, and friendship.

Aaron Aviles

Adam Joosten

Adam Steiner

Alexia Grevious

Alicia Rickter Piazza

Alisa Jacobs

Amanda Rodrigues

Andreas Johansson

Andrew "Bergie" Bergman

Andrew Giuliani

Andrew Goldberg

Andrew and Stacy Greenhut

Andrew Mirken

Andy Eminger

Andy and Sandy Quiroz

Anthony Pitts, Jr.

Anthony Josephedes

Art Aaronson

Bari Lovi

Barry Bookhard

Barry Dakake

Barry Katz

Ben Litvin

Ben Sturner

Beth Howell

Beth Ravin

Bill Meade

Bill Mount

Bill Snouffer

Bill Williams

Bob Mcgee

Bob Rose

Bob Shami

Brad Cohen

Brandon and Daniel
Rubenstein

Brian Harrington

Brian Samuels

Bruce Ampolsky

Bruce Lipnick

The Caiza Family (Hilda,
Patrick, and Jennifer)

Aunt Carol Feltman

Cam Fordham

Carrie Zelman Burlock

Caryn Mendez

Charles Smith

Chris Amoroso

Chris Butler

Chris Cuomo

Chris Gialanella

Chris Iannone

Chris Morrow

Chris and Liz Mullin

Chris Van Bard

Christina Francis

Clyde Drexler

Colby Estes

Cora Strahman Porter

Senator Cory Booker

Cousin Dean and
Neil Eisenberg

Cousin Elizabeth and
Stephanie Prince

Cousin Laura and Sheila

Craig Bulkum

Cynthia "Cindi" Montgomery

Dan Agatino

Dan Wulkan

Dana Pump

Dana Strum

Dara Cohen

Darek Robinson

Darren Rovell

Darryl Strawberry

Dave Glaskin/ Judy Katz

Dave Grutman

David Dillon

Dean Faragi

Dean and AG Spanos

Deborah Morales

Denise Menz

Dennis "Denny
     Moe" Mitchell

Derek Frazier

Dina Shapiro

Dr. Drew Pinsky

Dr. Kevin Drumbore

Dr. Michael Canella

Dr. Rob Destafano

Donald Osborne

Donna Greco

Donna Kurtzer

Dorna Taylor

Doug Bopst

Doug Keene

Doug Lawson

Doug Shabelman

Dustin Warburton

Eddie Fernandez

Elis Pacheco

Elizabeth Rosenthal Traub

Emma Goldsmith Dempster

Eric Amgar

Eric Galen

Eric Holoman

Erica Coburn

Erynn Joi

Estee Portney

Eugene Evans

Floyd Raglin

Fran Cunningham

Fran Judkins

Frank and Sheila Daukis

Frank Weimann

Fred and Patty Fogg

Found Vegas (Alex, John,
     Ethan, and Tom)

Gabe Catalano

Richard and Gail Singer

Gary Dell'abate

Giancarlo Funicello

Gigi

Gary and Weatta Collins

Gary Takahashi

George Kohler

Gena Lee Nolin-Hulse

Gerena and Suzette Garrido
     and family

Glenn Firestone

Glenn "GG" Gulino

Gloria Borges

Greg Drucks

Harvey Levin and Dennis
     Broad (TMZ)

Heather Frieman

Heather Halpern Rabinowitz

Hugo Dooner

Jane Beup

James Fox

James Luna

Jared Lerner

Jared Weiss

JB Bernstein

Jeffrey Davis

Jeffrey Krantz

Jeff Scher

Jeremy Nachtigal

Jerry Cohen

Jerry Rice

Jesse Katz and Roots of
    Fight Family

Jessica Panes

Jigar Thakarar

Jill Muller

Jim and Chris Click

Jimmy Spence

Joe and Melissa Gorga

Joe Natale

Johanna Martin

Jon Morgenthau

John Alvino

John Clancy, Jr.

John Doleva

John Formica

John King

John Saraceno

John Zinnman

Jonny Katz

Jeff Lutes

Jerry Doppelt

Jim Honobach

Joel Alpert

Joey Morrissey

Joseph Sozzani

Judy O'Connor

Judy Simon

Julius "Dr. J" Erving

Justin Dennis

Kawanna Brown

Keith Benson

Kelly Knievel

Kelvin Joseph

Kenny Pearson

Kevin Byrd

Kit Young

Krystal Knievel

Les Wolf

Lidia Pearl

Lisa Perlmutter Gold

Lisa Sadeghian

Liz Mullin (Sports
    Business Journal)

Lou Cavallo

Lyssee Graber Trachtman

Marc Garfinkle

Marc NehAmen

Marcus and Susanna Stern

Mark Adrian

Mark Murphy

Mark Schwartz

Marko Joyner

Marti Ruiz

Marty Mazza

Marvis Frazier

Matt Endlich

Matt Israel

Matt Lalin

Matt Posner

Matt Schumann

Mayi Araya

Mercedes Cisneros

Meredith Shapiro Deutsch

Michael and Judy Dancy

Michael Levine

Miguel Ramos

Mike "Smoothie" Erber

Mike Heller

Mike Mcgrath

"Iron" Mike Mears

Mike Silver

"Iron" Mike Tyson

Mike Walters

Misty Sacapano

My Aussie sisters, Mariam
     Freig, Sylvia So, Sneki

Bjelic ,and Nada
     Sefian Gaona

Nicole Forige

Nikkole Denson

Oscar Ulloa

Pamela Anderson

Pat Tortorello

Patrick Corridon

Paul Goldstein

Paul Meyers

Peter Berger

Peter Conti

Peter Hecht

Peter Ginopolis

Phyllis Lacca

R. Couri Hay

Renae Martin

Rich Altman

Richard and Kitt Greenberg

Richard Johnson

Richard Kurdek

Rick Vrablik

Rick Farrow

Rhona Graff

Rob Tolstoi

Robert and Trish Del Russo

Robert Detore

Robin Roth

Rocco Buonvino

Ron Howard

Ronn Torossian

Ross Foreman

Roy and Lori Goderstad

Russ LaFreniere

Ryan Wilichinsky

Sam Younes

Sasha Taylor

Scott Allen

Scott Dior

Scott Mahlum and
    Brent Holcomb

Scott Miller

Scottie Schwartz

Sean Jacoby

Shannon Barr

Sharon Bell

Sharron Pearson

Shayne Schloo

Sheila Ewing

Sheila Marquart

Sherie Wagner Douglas

Spud Webb

Stacy Royal

Stan Kay

Stephanie Dellisanti

Stephen Shamis

Steve "Drama" Donahue

Steve Lynskey

Steve Graus

Steve Grad

Steve Kessler

Steve Sussmann

Susan Kruger

Suzanne Alworth

Terry McCartney

Tina Cancellieri

Tom and Laura Berenger

Tom Tevlin

Tommy Iorio

Tommy Unger

Tony Todd

Trish Del Russo

Troy Berry

Vanessa Prieto

Vince Neil

Wass Stevens

William Castleberry

And a special love/shout out to my San Diego Chargers (LA Chargers), Boston Bruins, 1980s Boston Celtics, Grateful Dead, Mookie Wilson/1986 NY Mets, and *Three's Company*, the TV show.